Prep
+
Rally

Prep + Rally

AN HOUR OF PREP,
A WEEK OF DELICIOUS MEALS

———————

DINI KLEIN

HARVEST

An Imprint of WILLIAM MORROW

FIRST EDITION

Photography by Ren Fuller
Design and line art by Jennifer Chung

Library of Congress Cataloging-in-Publication Data
has been applied for.

ISBN 978-0-358-64556-6

22 23 24 25 26 TC 10 9 8 7 6 5 4 3 2 1

To Andi, Jolie, and Solomon

For all the "fums up" and happy dances, this book was made with you and for you. I'm the luckiest mama to have you three!

Contents

Part 3:
Extra Goodies: Recipes to Round Out Your Week and Use Up What's Left! 231

Introduction

My Aha Moment

While every parent believes that feeding their family is part of the job, feeding families literally *is* my job. Growing up, I always thought a career in fashion was my calling. After graduating from the Fashion Institute of Technology in New York City, I decided to completely pivot and become a private chef. While it may sound glamorous, it was incredibly taxing work; running around different grocery stores in all weather conditions, in and out of cabs, schlepping food up and down New York City apartments, prepping large menus for 25-person dinner parties, stocking fridges to accommodate special diets, and cooking for ultra-picky eaters. While the job itself was challenging, finding time to feed my own family proved even harder.

I struggled to balance cooking for my clients and getting a simple dinner on the table for my own family. I was just so tired of cooking. People always assumed that because of what I did, my own family must eat so well. But it was actually the opposite. You know how they say the shoemaker's kids have no shoes? It was that bad.

One day, as I was eating a bowl of cereal for dinner, it struck me like a ton of bricks: For some of my clients, I was prepping staple dishes that, with my direction, they would then mix and match to create different meals for the following few days. I had unwittingly created a system for my clients that could work for any family, especially my own. The solution was right in front of me all along.

I took it one step further and created smart meal prep menus consisting of staples that I could bang out on Sunday and then mix and match to feed my family throughout the week. I designed my meal plans to be most efficient, allowing me to shop once and get in and out of the kitchen in about an hour so that I could still enjoy my Sunday!

Roasted chicken, rice, and broccoli became chicken fried rice one day and chicken burritos the next. Why would we eat the same food each day if I could reinvent those staples into different dinners every night? It saved time and loads of money, and I loved the creative process of giving leftovers a new life. I suddenly had a happy and well-fed family and young kids who were all great eaters. The constant switch-up and variety of food was their normal, which made them always up for trying new things. They also loved getting involved in the process of cooking or even assembling a DIY-style dinner with those staples. It only got sweeter when I realized that even *Mike* (my husband) could assemble the staple dishes for our family and serve dinner with just my written instructions. (This is a man who rotates between cereal, yogurt, and an occasional egg when asked for something to eat. We all have our strengths!)

It occurred to me that if this system worked for my family, it could also work for other busy families frantically getting through the busy workweek.

Prep + Rally was born.

The Prep + Rally Way

In 2018, I left private cheffing because I knew this newfound system could help far more people. Since then, the Prep + Rally digital meal prep system has helped feed thousands of busy families throughout the week. With a well-thought-out game plan you can *Prep* staple recipes and meal components on Sunday and then *Rally* by creating quick, delicious meals using those Prep recipes. This helps you get through the week with extra time, more money in your pocket, and less stress about what to feed your family.

I've taken my method and poured it into these pages to show you how meal planning can de-stress your week and feed your family with minimal time, effort, and money. My hope is to give you the tools to become a savvier cook so that you can enjoy different meals every single night with a little creativity and thoughtfulness heading into the week. With a mix of classic kid favorites and some new soon-to-be favorites, I can assure you that each recipe is flavorful, simple to make, and smart/

efficient in the way it's prepared. It will also inspire you to repurpose items in a whole new way.

You'll notice that one dish can feel elevated for the grown-ups and can be tweaked simply to appeal to the kiddos. You don't need to eat chicken nuggets or plain noodles just because you have kids. We will change that.

This isn't a diet meal prep book, nor is it geared toward a specific way of eating. One quick "meal prep" Google search turns up many keto, weight loss, vegan, and paleo books and services. But how about the people who need this most: PARENTS! This method is about feeding your family wholesome, crowd-pleasing meals that are easily modified as desired to work for everyone.

You won't find anything complicated here, or recipes that require too many steps. My goal wasn't to reinvent the wheel, rather to create a better wheel. I wanted the recipes to be somewhat familiar but prepared in a more efficient way. I tested out giant dumplings and even Indian dosas but immediately nixed them because we just don't have time for that, *am I right*? I wanted every recipe to be practical, versatile, and an all-around crowd-pleaser. I had all my kids taste-test every single item in this book and kept tweaking the recipes based on their feedback. Of course Mike got some say as well, because I want adults to enjoy these meals just as much as the kids do. He's usually the toughest critic of all, and although I sometimes hate the honesty, it really served me here.

I love drawing inspiration from around the world and re-creating recipes that I know will be family-friendly. In these pages, I share my shortcuts and modifications to traditional recipes in the hopes of getting dinner on the table stress-free. I hope to inspire you in the kitchen, spark your creativity, and show you that you can:

- Eat like a grown-up even if you have kids.
- Learn to repurpose leftovers to reduce waste and create fun new meals.
- Do a little prep at the start of the week to save time and stress.
- Save money by shopping once for the whole week ahead.
- Gain the confidence to start cooking without a recipe and balance flavors on your own.
- Learn to cook in a thoughtful order to maximize time in the kitchen and minimize mess.

- Modify meal plans and learn to create your own menus.
- Make one dinner for your whole family, with some creative modifications to please everyone.

Let's just say you can have it *all*, and I'm here to teach you the tricks of the trade. I believe that feeding your family shouldn't consume you. With a smart plan in place, and armed with the tools to get the job done, you can enjoy your week the way *you* choose.

I'm here to take away the stress that too often accompanies meal preparation and show you how to Prep + Rally!

PART 1

The Prep + Rally Method

Diving In

This is the book I wish I'd had years ago when I was so burned out from working all week that I found myself eating cereal for dinner and stressing about how to cook for my growing family. Discovering how to Prep + Rally has changed my life in so many ways—it's taken away the stress of meal planning, grocery shopping, and getting dinner on the table. It's made cooking fun again, and freed up time and energy for me to actually enjoy meals with my family. And I know it can do the same for you!

How exactly do you Prep + Rally? The method is simple, and it's all about making dinner easier and more efficient. I've designed weekly grocery lists and meal plans for four weeknight dinners. Designate one day a week for **Prep**, when you'll cook all the staple recipes and prepare components for the four meals. In just about one hour of prep, you set yourself up for a week of success! Then pick four nights of the week to **Rally**, which is when you take staple recipes and meal components from your Prep and transform them into flavorful and balanced meals. I like to Prep on Sunday and Rally Monday through Thursday, leaving the weekends open for repurposing leftovers, going out, or dinner on the fly.

HOW TO PREP + RALLY

- **Shop:** Each meal plan includes a customizable grocery list and family-friendly menu. Shop for the groceries, and go into the week with a plan.
- **Prep:** I'll guide you through this recipe by recipe, with helpful tips along the way. With just about an hour of prep, you'll be ready to go into the week feeling confident.
- **Rally:** Congrats! You've got an array of dishes prepped, sorted, and ready to transform into four delicious dinners to enjoy in minutes.

I've designed this book so you can use it for weekly meals and to serve as a general guide for efficiency in the kitchen, allowing you to save time, money, and sanity. New to meal prep? Don't be intimidated! Tackling a full-on meal prep may seem daunting at first. You may think you're not a meal planning kind of person. I hear it all the time, and I didn't think I was that person either. To be honest, some weeks I'm not! That's why there are so many ways to use this book and make the Prep + Rally system your own.

You can go all in by shopping the grocery list for the week ahead and cooking the dinners each night as you go through the week. Four dinners too much this week? Make two instead. The grocery list and Prep recipes are all designed for modification. I sometimes bang out the Prep just to have some great staples stashed away in the fridge and then serve them as is, allowing everyone to make their own meal to suit themselves. Maybe you'll select one chicken recipe to batch cook and use it two different ways throughout the week. Or perhaps you'll just choose one recipe from the book to cook for a single night's dinner.

Some people prefer food that is cooked the day it's served, and that's always an option too. You can prep items and store them so that all you have to do is throw them in the oven the day you want to serve them. Simply having your shopping done on Sunday and a plan for the week ahead is enough for some people. And if Sundays don't work for you to Prep, go ahead and bang it out

on a Monday when the house is quiet—I do this all the time! Cook your way through these menus any way that works for *you*.

No matter which journey you choose, remember that it's yours and it's supposed to make your life simpler. There is zero pressure and no shame, and you should never feel any guilt. Our goal as busy parents during these child-rearing years is to simply survive the madness and keep the tiny humans alive, healthy, happy, and fed while still enjoying the beautiful journey. Boy, does it go fast! But if you're reading this . . . you're already on the right track.

How to Use This Book

The goal for this book was to create a resource for busy families and to create a helpful guide to de-stress dinner. I'm all about recipes that will appeal to kids while still being sophisticated enough for grown-ups. Feel free to go all in with the Prep + Rally meal plans, or start with a recipe or two and build up from there.

In part 1, I break down the basics of the Prep + Rally method, with my best tips for feeding the kiddos, food storage tips, and how to stock your kitchen for meal prep success.

In part 2, I share ten all-new Prep + Rally weekly meal plans, complete with a weekly grocery list, Prep recipes, and four complete Rally meals for each plan. The menus are designed to feed a family of four, but you can always modify by scaling up or down as needed. There are meal plans for every palate and mood, from "Spiced and Stewed" to "No Way It's Veg," "Winter Cozies," and "Nostalgic Magic." You can tackle a full Prep + Rally meal plan or pick a meal à la carte. This book is all about making the method work for you, so have fun with it!

Each meal plan includes Hot Tips and Rally Remedies with ways to modify the recipes for vegetarians, dietary preferences, allergies, and picky eaters. My menus consist of recipes for wholesome dishes that everyone can enjoy as written or with minor tweaks. These menus are infinitely versatile, so you can truly make them yours and choose your own adventure every time you revisit them. I want you to keep opening this book for inspiration and to learn to think about meal preparation in a whole new way.

Each Prep + Rally menu includes:

- An outline of the four dinner menus for the week (Monday to Thursday, or any four days you choose).
- A grocery list, noting which ingredients correspond with each Rally menu, and which are for Prep instead of Rally.
- Your Prep list: 7 to 8 recipes or staple dishes to prep and store for the week.
- Hot Tips and swap-out options for modifying each recipe.
- Your Rally recipes: Simple instructions on how to use your Prep recipes to Rally and create four unique dinners during the week.
- Rally Remedies to help you adjust the menus to accommodate various dietary needs and preferences.

In part 3, I share some of my favorite easy and essential recipes that can save lunch, dinner, or even snack time any day of the week. In "Leftover Remix" (page 235), I've included my best tips and recipes for repurposing leftovers. These recipes are so fresh and creative, you'd never guess they were sourced from those leftovers languishing in the fridge! I hope the leftovers section gives you some great meals you'll cook again and again, but also serves as inspiration for those times you just want to chuck that leftover quinoa or those last few pieces of broccoli! This section is great to visit on Friday or Saturday when you're looking to revamp leftovers from the week into a quick, new meal.

In "Last-Minute Scramble" (page 261), I've included recipes built on the foundation of the ultimate dinner saver, eggs. Eggs are always stocked in my fridge—I have three dozen on hand at any given time! I truly believe they're the perfect last-minute dinner when you just don't have anything else. They're versatile; can make a complete meal in just minutes; can be served for breakfast, lunch, or dinner; and just about everyone loves them. We usually do eggs for dinner on Sunday to keep things simple and healthy while I meal prep for the week ahead.

What's a cookbook without a sweet ending? In "Sweets, Snacks, and Everything in Between," I've rounded up all our simple family-favorite treats. There are lots of prep-ahead recipes (Don't we all love a breakfast we can grab on the go?) and dishes you can switch up to utilize ingredients you already have at home.

At the end of the book, I share some mix-and-match ideas (page 296) using the recipes in the book, plus a DIY Prep + Rally tutorial (page 297) that makes it easy for you to create your own weekly meal plans.

Tips on Feeding Tiny Humans

I hear it all the time: "My kids are so picky! How do you get yours to eat so well? I can never cook real food because all they want are basic kid dinners!"

Kids are tough. And the longer they're accustomed to a certain lifestyle, the harder it is to switch things up. But with some small tweaks and helpful tips, I believe we can always improve the situation.

The first thing is to stop throwing your dinner needs on the back burner because you don't think your kids will eat your "grown-up" meal. You are important and deserve to eat well! You don't need to eat leftover noodles for dinner just because that's what the kids ate and it's convenient. Let's get ahead of the situation and make everyone happy, right?

Menu Selection

Pick out a menu (or even one recipe that can be repurposed into another the next day) and review it with your crew. Omit anything that definitely won't work for your family and tweak others to make it more appealing to them. Perhaps they'll eat plain smash burgers (see page 178), while the grown-ups get burgers with the spice coating. You can always skip some steps to simplify a recipe for the picky ones.

Make It Fun

Have the kids come to the grocery store with you or help pick out groceries online to save even more time. Pick out some fun desserts for post-dinner treats. Buy buns or tacos to make the meals more kid-friendly. Buy cookie cutters to make shapes out of veggies. Try skewers to make kebabs. Decorative plates and even chopsticks always make dinner more fun. If your kids like to keep busy, choose one of the many menus that has a DIY component, like building your own taco or making your own hot pot. Just add a little pizzazz into the mix!

Never Push Too Hard

New food can be totally scary for kids. Sometimes just getting them to try one bite and then allowing them to choose if they want more is a victory. Show them how happy you are that they tried something you worked hard to make, then try again next time. It can take trying something a few times, in different versions and with various textures, to finally enjoy a food. For example, my kids still refuse to eat cauliflower rice, but they devour cauliflower florets. Just keep at it!

This Is Dinner

Let your kids know this is what's for dinner. It's not a yogurt or cereal. Once they know that those other options are not available, they may be more open to eating the dinner you prepared. Remember, you're the boss. They can't eat frozen pizza and nuggets if it's not in the freezer! Show them all the fun ways they can customize their meal to make it their own, which instills confidence and fosters creativity. They will feel like they're making all the choices when really, you've determined what's for dinner—they just get to choose how to eat it. Smart, huh?

Remember, They Can Make Some Choices Too

Kids are also human, and they should have the power to decide if they're full, or if they want one last bite. Give them the confidence to make decisions for themselves. It will serve them well for the rest of their lives. If they don't want to try something, that's okay too. Try again next time! Not every dinner will be a win, and going in with that assurance helps us feel less disappointed.

Set an Example

Kids replicate everything we do. And did you ever notice how your kid sometimes won't touch a certain food when you offer it, yet they'll try it when they're with a friend or with your spouse? It's all about the context and setting. Your goal is to always show them healthy eating habits. Make it a positive experience, and just have fun! This phase won't last forever, and remember, it's totally normal. Just do your best.

Storing Your Food

Given that this book is all about prepping and storing meals for the week, here are my best tips for keeping your food fresh and safe to eat.

- Cooked food should be cooled right away and refrigerated or frozen within 2 hours of being cooked. That means you should try to cool everything down completely and get it in the fridge right away when you've finished your meal prep.
- I store most of my meal prep items in airtight glass storage containers. Having less contact with air will keep your food fresher longer, and glass storage containers allow you to see what you have in your fridge!
- Label and date your containers. It helps you stay organized and prioritize leftovers.
- Fish should be eaten 1 to 2 days after it's cooked for optimal freshness. You'll notice it's always on the first night's Rally menu in the Prep + Rally plans.
- Cooked chicken and meat can be stored in the fridge for up to 4 days for safest consumption.

- Cooked grains and veggies can be kept in the fridge for up to 5 days.
- Dressing and sauces are my favorite part of Sunday meal prep, as they will keep for anywhere from 1 to 2 weeks in an airtight jar in the fridge!
- Too much food? Generally soups, most proteins, casseroles, and desserts all freeze beautifully. I like to keep grains and veggies fresh!
- When freezing, make sure the food is completely cooled so the moisture doesn't cause ice crystals inside and ruin the contents. You also don't want to warm and ruin other food in the freezer.
- Whenever I freeze a cake, I wrap it in a layer of plastic wrap and then a layer of aluminum foil to give it extra protection from the freezer. Muffins and cookies I just store in Stasher silicone storage bags or resealable plastic bags.

Stock Up for Success

You can't start Rallying before you Prep, and I strongly advise doing a little prep for your Prep! Here are all the kitchen essentials I reach for most often. I've included staples that are great to keep on hand for quick last-minute meals and for repurposing yesterday's dinner. I've also included all my favorite quick flavor boosters so you can get a restaurant-quality dish for a fraction of the effort and cost. We're learning to think smart, spend less, and enjoy more time *out* of the kitchen!

FREEZER

EGG ROLL WRAPPERS: My go-to when I'm in need of a last-minute dinner. I make egg rolls with just about anything left over from the week.

FROZEN VEGETABLES: I love keeping peas, edamame, broccoli, and spinach stocked in my freezer to make soup, to throw into a last-minute meal, or as a quick side dish.

MEAT, CHICKEN, AND FISH: Always a good idea to keep on hand to avoid extra trips to the butcher or fishmonger.

PIE DOUGH: My favorite way to make a quick chicken potpie with leftover chicken or a sweet or savory galette.

PIZZA DOUGH: When in doubt, throw it on a pizza. You can buy dough from your local pizza shop (like we do) or the grocery store and freeze it. You can even buy precooked pizza crusts to make things simpler.

PUFF PASTRY: The fastest way to use up leftover meat or vegetables or even turn out quick appetizers.

PANTRY

ALLIUMS: Onions, chives, and scallions are my top choices.

CANNED BEANS AND LENTILS: These are always in my pantry for last-minute veggie burgers.

CANNED CHIPOTLE PEPPERS IN ADOBO SAUCE AND/OR DRIED CALIFORNIA CHILES: My absolute favorite spicy/smoky flavor boosters that give life to shakshuka and add depth to any sauce or salsa.

GARLIC: I grew up with fresh garlic in my backyard garden, so whenever possible I use fresh. The tighter the head, the more potent the cloves.

HOT SAUCE: I add hot sauce to just about everything. Cholula is my favorite of the bunch.

KOSHER SALT AND PEPPER: The pillars of any good dish, and the secret to making your food go from okay to great. Season, taste, season, taste. I always use Morton kosher salt in my house, and it's what I used to test all the recipes in this book. You'll also notice most of the recipes say to add salt and pepper to taste. That's because I want the seasoning to be right for you and to build your confidence in the kitchen by getting into the habit of tasting as you cook. It's the only way to truly make great food.

MAPLE SYRUP AND HONEY: A touch of sweetness takes a dish from great to fabulous and when it's a natural sweetener, you can feel good about adding it. I buy them in bulk, as you'll notice I like to use these sweeteners in most of my baked goods and even in my daily coffee.

MARINARA SAUCE: I buy canned Don Pepino brand pizza sauce in bulk online and use it any time a recipe calls for marinara sauce or crushed tomatoes. Their sauce tastes like you cooked fresh tomato sauce from scratch. It's truly the best.

MISO: Nothing gives a dish that salty, umami-rich flavor quite like miso. You can find it in many grocery stores nowadays, or just order it online. It's not a necessity, but miso packs mega flavor and is one of my favorite ingredients to keep on hand. Plus, it lasts a long time in the fridge.

NUT BUTTER: A creamy foundation for sauces and dressings. I only buy natural butters with no added sugar. Read your labels carefully!

NUTS AND SEEDS: The base for vegan creamy sauces, salad toppers to add texture, and pesto builders. Store these in the fridge or freezer once opened to retain freshness and keep them from going rancid. I always toast them before adding them to my food (see page 144 for directions). It's an extra step, but makes a huge difference in flavor and texture.

OIL: I mostly use olive oil in my kitchen. I use light olive oil for roasting, sautéing, and sometimes even baking. I use good-quality extra-virgin olive oil for dressings and sauces that are uncooked. Grapeseed and avocado oil are great neutral cooking oils (as I refer to them throughout this book) for cooking at higher temperature and frying. I always recommend buying oil spray for roasting and achieving even coverage. You can also purchase oil sprayer bottles, which is less expensive and less wasteful than replacing the single-use spray bottles every time.

PANKO BREAD CRUMBS: Turn any vegetable into a crisp, dunkable fry or give fish a crispy exterior for an irresistible dinner. Get a quick flavor bonus by buying flavored crumbs.

PASTA: An obvious staple that every family has on hand. Pasta is the perfect base for any meal, and it's great for using up leftover vegetables or protein from the week. It's a pantry staple that pleases all.

RICE AND QUINOA: We make a big batch of rice or quinoa at the start of the week and it serves as different lunches and dinners all week long.

SEAWEED SNACKS: My kids love these as a snack, and they find their way into many of my recipes. I love the salty crispiness they bring to a dish.

SPICES: I have way too many spices at home, but the ones I reach for most often are garlic powder, onion powder, oregano, chili powder, cumin, and curry powder.

SOY SAUCE/TAMARI: One of my favorite ingredients for marinades and dressing. I always buy low-sodium soy sauce and tamari, and that's what all the recipes in this book were tested with.

TAHINI: Creates instant creamy dressings or sauces and is also great for sweet dishes like oatmeal. Double whammy.

FRIDGE

CAPERS: Little briny nuggets of goodness. Love these guys in pastas, chicken, fish, and salads. Chop them up to make them less noticeable for kids.

CHEESE: I keep mozzarella and Parmesan on hand at all times.

COCONUT MILK: Canned coconut milk keeps forever in the pantry and gives a luscious finish to any sauce, marinade, or stew.

DIJON MUSTARD: A great emulsifier and flavor booster for dressings.

EGGS: Sweet, savory, whipped, scrambled, poached . . . the sky's the limit with eggs. That's why I devoted a whole section in this book to them.

FRESH CITRUS: This is one thing I'm a snob about. Bottled lemon and lime juices taste like a cleaning product to me, and they completely ruin food. Don't do it! Buy fresh lemons and limes in bulk to always have on hand. They last a long time in the fridge.

GREEK YOGURT/SOUR CREAM: Great base for a delicious sauce or crema.

HERBS: When looking to wake up any dish or add gorgeous color and flavor, look no further than fresh herbs. So many varieties, and all beautiful notes of flavor. Wash them right when you bring them home from the grocery store, dry well (I love to do this in a salad spinner), and store in a sealed glass jar to increase their shelf life.

OLIVES AND PEPPERONCINI: The fastest way to get a punch of tang, saltiness, and acid.

SUN-DRIED TOMATOES PACKED IN OIL: I use the oil in dressings (there's an insane amount of flavor in there, so don't throw it out) and the actual tomatoes in salads, pastas, chicken salads, etc.

TOFU: It lasts a very long time in the fridge and makes the perfect last-minute meal. My kids love it simply drained, dried, cubed, and roasted with salt and oil until crispy.

TORTILLAS: Just about anything can be repurposed when rolled up in a tortilla, and there are endless ways to use them. We are obsessed with almond flour tortillas in our house.

VINEGAR: Acid is essential to balancing flavor. Rice vinegar, red wine vinegar, balsamic vinegar, distilled white vinegar, and apple cider vinegar are all great. These are the vinegars I keep stocked in my pantry and use daily, and they can almost always be used interchangeably.

Essential Kitchen Tools

AIRTIGHT STORAGE CONTAINERS: I opt for glass containers because I can store, heat, and serve all in the same dish. I also like that I can see through them and keep track of what I have in my fridge. I use BPA-free plastic containers for storing cooked pastas, salads, and cut-up fruit.

CHEF'S KNIFE: Every kitchen needs a good sharp chef's knife. There is never a need to buy a whole knife set. I recommend buying one or two good-quality chef's knives that you love and that feel comfortable in your hand. Go to the store and try them on for size! You can spend $100 and get a great knife that will last you for years. Take care of it and keep it sharp. I use a two-stage handheld knife sharpener to easily sharpen mine whenever it feels dull.

CITRUS REAMER: You can get the clamp kind or a simple wooden reamer. I use mine daily!

CUTTING BOARDS: You can't tackle meal prep without a great work surface. I use a lightweight wooden cutting board with a handle (like on the Prep + Rally Board) for vegetable prep, a separate cheaper plastic cutting board for cutting protein (I replace this every few months), and another wooden one just for cutting fruit so the fruit doesn't end up tasting like onions or garlic.

FINE-MESH SIEVE: Such a great tool for removing ingredients from boiling water, straining sauces, and rinsing grains. I like a larger one that's big enough to fit at least two cups of grains for rinsing all at once.

GARLIC PRESS: Saves time mincing and spares your cutting board from stink.

HIGH-SPEED BLENDER: Best for making smoothies and sauces completely smooth and creamy. Even the kids won't find the spinach in that smoothie. I've had my Vitamix for nine years and have found it completely worth the investment.

ICE CREAM SCOOP: I use this scoop to make pancakes, muffins, latkes, burgers, etc. Basically everything but ice cream!

IMMERSION BLENDER: While I love a high-speed blender for smoothies, an immersion blender is my essential tool for blending soups and sauces. By blending these directly in the soup pot or wide-mouthed storage container, you're able to save loads of time and dishes.

INSTANT-READ DIGITAL THERMOMETER: There's just no other way to be completely confident your proteins are fully cooked and not overcooked. Invest in this $5 tool and stop guessing. Trust me!

MICROPLANE: For zesting ginger, garlic, lemons, and limes. It's hard to match the fresh flavor of citrus zest, and a Microplane simplifies the task.

NUT-MILK BAG AND SALAD SPINNER: Not a must, but these tools are great for squeezing extra moisture out of spinach (great for my Spinach Galette, page 252), eggplant (see page 195), zucchini (see page 292), and chickpeas (page 34) prior to cooking, resulting in crispier food. A salad spinner is also great for drying herbs—and lettuce, of course.

PARCHMENT PAPER: I use parchment paper to line my sheet pans simply because it makes cleanup so much easier. And if you can buy ready-cut sheets that are the exact size of your pan, it makes life a heck of a lot easier!

POTS AND PANS: At a minimum, every kitchen should have both an 8-inch and a 10-inch skillet in ceramic/nonstick material. You should also have some stainless-steel pots and pans, including an 8-quart stockpot and 2- and 4-quart saucepans. A heavy-bottomed enameled Dutch oven is a great investment as well, and will last you a lifetime.

SALAD CHOPPER: I love using this handy-dandy tool not only to make quick and easy salads without a cutting board, but also for blending burger mixtures, meat loaf, and mashing bananas for banana bread.

SHEET PANS: These are the most essential meal-prepping tool, right after the knife and cutting board. I recommend buying 3 or 4 (20 x 14 inch) extra-large baking sheets (USA Pan is my favorite brand, and the best when meal prepping in bulk). If you prefer the standard sheet pan, go for four of five half sheet pans (13 x 18 inches) for cooking absolutely everything (you'll see me referring to these as "standard baking sheets" in the recipes). It's also good to have 1 or 2 quarter sheet pans (9 x 13) for making bars and desserts.

SILICONE PRODUCTS: I love Stasher silicone storage bags for packing school snacks in addition to storing ingredients in my fridge, freezer, and pantry. Food Huggers are great for storing leftover produce and covering your storage containers. Souper Cubes are the best for freezing canned goods left over from your prep (coconut milk, crushed tomatoes, etc.) to avoid waste, and freezing your soups and stews in blocks saves space in your freezer. Silicone baking cups can be found on Amazon; they are not only eco-friendly, but they keep your muffins and egg cups from sticking to the muffin tin. Plus, the kids like to use them in their lunch boxes to section out their snacks!

WHISK: I use a whisk whenever I mix together pancake batter, cake or muffin batter, dressings, etc. It helps you get a completely smooth consistency and ensures everything is fully incorporated. There's nothing worse than biting into a blob of baking soda—I know you know what I'm talking about! Put that whisk to work.

WIDE-MOUTHED MASON JARS: For prepping and storing dressings. I like wide-mouthed jars, in a variety of sizes, because they fit the head of the immersion blender so you can blend and store in the same container. Le Parfait and Weck brand jars are my favorites. I recommend buying four 16-ounce jars and four 32-ounce jars with lids.

Not exactly a tool, but the **CONVECTION ROAST SETTING** on the oven is one of the best-kept secrets in the kitchen. Not every oven has a convection setting (which is why the recipes in this book were written for the standard bake setting), but I find that even people whose ovens *do* have it don't know about it. Convection is best for browning and roasting food quickly, leaving roasted vegetables golden and crisping the skin on roasted chicken without drying out the bird. Essentially, on the convection setting, a fan in the oven circulates the hot air, helping food cook faster and more evenly, and drying the food's exterior, allowing it to become crisp! By cooking food faster, you're also able to more efficiently get through your meal prep!

Always decrease the oven temperature in the recipe by about 25°F when using the convection setting, as it cooks more rapidly than the regular bake setting. Additionally, even if the recipe calls for a specific cook time, you should always be checking the oven periodically, as everyone's oven heats differently and food cooks differently depending on which oven rack it's on. Get to know your oven and become friends with it. And definitely start using the convection roast setting for all your savory cooking. When roasted vegetables are cooked to perfection, your family will start craving them—absolutely addicting!

PART 2

Let's
Prep + Rally

The Weekly Meal Plans

Before You Prep

Get ready to revolutionize dinner with the Prep + Rally meal plans! Here are some helpful tips before you prep:

- These menus are meant to serve a family of four, so adjust accordingly.
- The number on each grocery list corresponds to the numbered Prep recipe so that you can easily nix or swap out grocery items as needed.
- The "R" on each grocery list points out which items will be used to Rally (or serve) later in the week. No need to have those ingredients out during your Prep, but be sure to shop for them.
- You'll find lots of swaps at the start of each meal plan so that you can adjust your menu according to your dietary restrictions or preferences.
- The Hot Tips sprinkled throughout the recipes offer loads of cooking tricks and serving ideas.
- The Rally Remedies give you different ways to modify each dinner to please everyone.

Feeling ready? Here are a few additional helpful bits to make your meal prep more efficient and fun:

- Pull everything out of the fridge and give the shelves a quick wipe-down. Take inventory of what you have (check those expiration dates!), then go ahead and reorganize the contents. I love doing this before I place my grocery order and proceed with my weekly meal prep, as it reduces waste and allows me to go into the week with a clear head. I get the kids involved in this process too!
- Place a garbage bin next to your workstation to avoid multiple trips.
- Wash all your produce before you start to save time.
- Set out all your cookware and ingredients before getting started.
- Dial up the tunes and recruit a cooking buddy.
- Grab that wine and get prepping!

CHAPTER 1

Spiced *and* Stewed

MAKES: 4 DINNERS, FOR 4 PEOPLE

This menu is a winner because it's simple yet incredibly bold in flavor. I've included many shortcuts to make the meal prep even less time-consuming, so hopefully you'll always be able to find some time to bang this one out. There's no such thing as cheating when it comes to meal prepping. Do what works for *you* and what makes your week easier. This menu is a great place to start if you're a meal-prepping newbie. Jump on in, my friend!

THIS WEEK'S MENU

- **BBQ Chicken** *with* **Chili-Spiced Sweet Potatoes** *and* **Zucchini**

- **Squash-Lentil Soup** *with* **Crispy Curried Chickpeas** *and* **Broccoli**

- **Chicken-Broccoli Egg Rolls** *with* **Ranch Dip** *and* **Roasted Zucchini**

- **Santa Fe Bowls**

PREP

1 **BBQ-Rubbed Chicken**

2 **Chili-Spiced Sweet Potatoes**

3 **Squash-Lentil Soup**

4 **Crispy Curried Chickpeas**

5 **Roasted Zucchini**

6 **Roasted Broccoli**

7 **Basic Quinoa**

8 **Ranch Dip**

NOTES & SWAPS

PREP SMART

- Save some time this week by buying store-bought ranch dressing.
- If you're really strapped for time, buy two store-bought rotisserie chickens instead of roasting your own. No shame in the game!

PREP IT MORE KID-FRIENDLY

- If your kids don't like chickpeas, feel free to make (or buy) garlic bread or croutons to top the soup instead.
- Serve Santa Fe Bowls with crunchy taco shells so the kids can have a taco night instead of salad. Let them have fun packing it with all the fillings they love.

PREP IT GLUTEN-FREE/LIGHTEN IT UP

- Make wraps instead of egg rolls! Buy some large tortillas (corn, flour, cassava, or almond tortillas all work), add shredded chicken in BBQ sauce along with the broccoli, some diced tomato, and shredded lettuce, and roll it up like a burrito. You can also serve the fillings in lettuce cups for an even lighter option. Serve with ranch dip for dunking.
- Prep cauliflower rice in place of quinoa.

PREP IT VEGETARIAN

- Coat tofu (or fish, to make it pescatarian) with BBQ spice rub and roast in place of the chicken.
- Instead of adding chicken to the egg rolls, make them vegetarian by sautéing an onion with some finely shredded cabbage, and add the broccoli and zucchini, all finely chopped. Season with extra BBQ spice rub and roll into egg rolls.

COOKING TOOLS AND EQUIPMENT NEEDED

- Chef's knife
- Cutting board
- 3 extra-large baking sheets or 4 or 5 standard baking sheets
- Large (6- to 8-quart) stockpot
- Immersion blender
- Medium (4-quart) saucepan
- Microplane
- Medium bowl
- 2 (16-ounce) wide-mouthed jars with lids

GROCERY LIST

PRODUCE
- 2 sprigs rosemary **2** **3**
- 3 large sweet potatoes **2**
- 1 onion **3**
- 9 medium zucchini **5**
- About 30 ounces (10 cups) broccoli florets **6**
- 2 lemons **3** **8** + 1 for R
- 1 garlic clove **8**
- 2 heads Bibb lettuce R
- 1 pint cherry tomatoes R

PANTRY
- Light olive oil
- Extra-virgin olive oil
- Kosher salt
- Pepper
- 1 tablespoon plus 2 teaspoons mild chili powder **1** **2**
- 1 teaspoon ground cumin **1**
- 2¾ teaspoons garlic powder **1** **4** **8**
- 2 teaspoons smoked paprika **1**
- 1 tablespoon plus 2¾ teaspoons onion powder **1** **2** **4** **8**
- 1 teaspoon dried oregano **2**
- ¾ teaspoon curry powder **4**
- ½ teaspoon dried parsley **8**
- ¾ cup dried red lentils **3**
- 32 ounces (4 cups) vegetable stock **3**
- 1 (28-ounce) can diced tomatoes **3**
- 2 (15.5-ounce) cans chickpeas **4**
- 1 cup quinoa **7**
- ¾ cup + 2 tablespoons mayonnaise **8**
- ¼ cup distilled white vinegar **8**
- 1 teaspoon Dijon mustard **8**
- Fresh loaf of bread or garlic bread R
- ½ cup BBQ sauce R

- 12 egg roll wrappers R
- 1 (15.5-ounce) can black beans R
- 1 (15.5-ounce) can corn kernels R
- Cooking oil spray R

DAIRY/FROZEN
- 1 cup Greek yogurt R
- 24 ounces (4 cups) frozen cubed butternut squash **3**

PROTEIN
- 2 whole chickens, each cut into 8 pieces, bone-in and skin-on **1**
- 4 large eggs R

*The "**R**" symbolizes ingredients you'll be using to Rally throughout the week—these won't be needed in the Sunday prep!

PREP

Time to prep! Set aside about an hour on your Prep day to make these recipes, then store them to use for Rally meals during the week.

1 BBQ-Rubbed Chicken

SERVES 4 PEOPLE FOR 2 MEALS

2 whole chickens, each cut into 8 pieces, bone-in and skin-on

1 tablespoon mild chili powder

1 tablespoon onion powder

1 tablespoon kosher salt

2 teaspoons garlic powder

2 teaspoons smoked paprika

1 teaspoon ground cumin

2 to 3 tablespoons light olive oil

1 Preheat the oven to 450°F. Line an extra-large baking sheet or two standard baking sheets with parchment paper. Arrange the chicken pieces in a single layer on the prepared pan(s).

2 In a small bowl, mix together the chili powder, onion powder, salt, garlic powder, paprika, and cumin, then sprinkle the spice mix evenly over the tops and bottoms of the chicken pieces. Drizzle the oil over the chicken and massage to coat, making sure to get under the skin too.

3 Roast, uncovered, on the top rack for about 50 minutes, until golden. Right when it comes out of the oven, transfer the chicken to a large storage container and pour the juices from the pan over the top. Let cool completely, then cover and store in the fridge.

HOT TIPS

• Triple or quadruple the BBQ rub spices, combine in a jar, and store for a quick rub anytime. It's great on fish, meat, chicken, and even veggies.

• To make this vegetarian, slice 3 (16-ounce) blocks of extra-firm tofu into cubes and dry them well with a clean kitchen towel. Coat the tofu liberally in the spice mixture and drizzle with the oil. Roast at 450°F for 15 to 20 minutes, until crisp and golden.

• If you're short on oven space and/or want an easier prep day, simply prep the chicken according to recipe directions and store to cook fresh prior to serving. You can do the same for any of the vegetables too!

• Switch this up by using thin-sliced boneless, skinless chicken breasts and grill on a grill pan.

2 Chili-Spiced Sweet Potatoes

SERVES 3 OR 4 PEOPLE FOR 2 MEALS

1 Preheat the oven to 450°F. Line an extra-large baking sheet or two standard baking sheets with parchment paper. Cut each sweet potato in half lengthwise. Cut each piece in half lengthwise again. Keep cutting until you have 1-inch wedges. Put the sweet potatoes on the prepared pan(s) and coat with the oil. Sprinkle with the chili powder, onion powder, oregano, rosemary, and salt and pepper to taste. Toss to combine and spread the sweet potatoes out on the pan(s) so none overlap.

2 Roast for about 45 minutes, until golden and crisp. Let cool, then store in the fridge.

3 large sweet potatoes, scrubbed

3 to 4 tablespoons light olive oil

2 teaspoons mild chili powder

1½ teaspoons onion powder

1 teaspoon dried oregano

1 sprig rosemary, minced (about 1 teaspoon)

Kosher salt and pepper

3 Squash-Lentil Soup

SERVES 6 TO 8

1 In a large stockpot, heat the oil over medium-high heat. Add the onion and cook until translucent. Add the squash, lentils, tomatoes, lemon zest and juice, rosemary, and stock. Season with salt and pepper. Bring to a boil, then reduce the heat to maintain a simmer, cover, and cook for 30 to 40 minutes. Season with additional salt and pepper as needed.

2 If desired, blend with an immersion blender until you've reached the desired consistency. Let cool, and store.

2 tablespoons light olive oil

1 onion, finely diced

4 cups frozen cubed butternut squash (24 ounces)

¾ cup dried red lentils

1 (28-ounce) can diced tomatoes

Zest and juice of 1 lemon

1 sprig rosemary, minced (about 1 teaspoon)

4 cups vegetable stock (32 ounces)

Kosher salt and pepper

HOT TIPS

- Feel free to use fresh butternut squash. I just love the convenience of frozen.

- If the soup gets too thick, add a splash of water or more stock to thin it out.

4 Crispy Curried Chickpeas

MAKES ABOUT 2 CUPS

2 (15.5-ounce) cans chickpeas, drained and rinsed

1 teaspoon onion powder

1 teaspoon kosher salt

¾ teaspoon curry powder

½ teaspoon garlic powder

1 tablespoon light olive oil

1 Preheat the oven to 450°F. Line a standard baking sheet with parchment paper.

2 Spread the chickpeas out on a clean kitchen towel. Fold the top half of the towel over the chickpeas and pat gently to thoroughly dry them. A salad spinner is another great way to dry chickpeas, if you have one!

3 Spread the chickpeas over the prepared baking sheet. Season with the onion powder, salt, curry powder, and garlic powder and drizzle with the oil. Massage to coat.

4 Roast on the center rack for about 35 minutes, shaking the pan halfway through, and cooking until super crunchy. Keep an eye on them at the end to avoid burning. Let cool completely, then store at room temperature in a glass storage container with a tight-fitting lid.

HOT TIPS

• If you have an air fryer, definitely utilize it here. It's the fastest method and makes for a super-crispy chickpea. Place spiced and oiled chickpeas in the air fryer basket and cook at 400°F for about 25 minutes or until golden.

• I've tried storing them many ways, and storing in an airtight glass jar on the counter makes for the longest shelf life. Avoid storing in a plastic bag.

• To save a step during your meal prep, either buy store-bought crunchy chickpeas or make them fresh later in the week.

5 Roasted Zucchini

SERVES 8

Preheat the oven to 450°F. Line one extra-large baking sheet or two standard baking sheets with parchment paper. Arrange the zucchini rounds on the prepared pan(s), drizzle with the oil, and season with salt and pepper. Toss to coat well. Spread the rounds out into a single layer. Roast, ideally on the top rack of the oven to encourage more browning, for about 30 minutes, until golden. Let cool, then store, covered, in the fridge.

9 medium zucchini, cut into rounds

2 to 3 tablespoons light olive oil

Kosher salt and pepper

HOT TIP

- If you don't have extra-large baking sheets (I highly recommend them, as they maximize space in the oven) or you don't have a second oven to fit everything at once, simply swap the baking sheets in and out of the oven as items are cooked. Alternatively, you can prep and cut the vegetables and store them to cook fresh later in the week.

6 Roasted Broccoli

SERVES 8

Preheat the oven to 450°F. Line an extra-large baking sheet or two standard baking sheets with parchment paper. Put the broccoli on the prepared pan(s), drizzle with the oil, season with salt and pepper, and toss to coat. Roast for 25 to 30 minutes until crisp and cooked through. Let cool, then store, covered, in the fridge.

10 cups broccoli florets (about 30 ounces)

2 to 3 tablespoons light olive oil

Kosher salt and pepper

7 Basic Quinoa

SERVES 4

1 cup quinoa

1¾ cups water

Pinch of kosher salt

In a medium or small saucepan, combine the quinoa, water, and salt. Bring to a boil over high heat, uncovered, then reduce the heat to maintain a simmer. Cover and cook for 10 minutes, until the water has been absorbed. Transfer to a storage container and let cool, then cover and store in the fridge.

HOT TIP

• Prep double the amount of quinoa to have extra for the week and to use for quick and easy grain bowls for lunch.

8 Ranch Dip

MAKES 1½ CUPS

¾ cup + 2 tablespoons mayonnaise

¼ cup distilled white vinegar

¼ cup extra-virgin olive oil

1 teaspoon Dijon mustard

1 garlic clove, minced

½ teaspoon dried parsley

¼ teaspoon onion powder

¼ teaspoon garlic powder

Zest and juice of 1 lemon (3 tablespoons juice)

Kosher salt and pepper

Combine the mayonnaise, vinegar, oil, mustard, garlic, parsley, onion powder, garlic powder, and lemon zest and juice in a tall storage jar. Cover with a tight-fitting lid and shake to mix. Season with salt and pepper as needed. Store in the fridge.

HOT TIP

• If you have any fresh herbs such as parsley or dill on hand, mince them and add them to the dip.

RALLY

Get ready to Rally! Time to take all those
Prep staples and use them to
create delicious meals for the week.

BBQ-Rubbed Chicken *with* Chili-Spiced Sweet Potatoes *and* Zucchini

SERVES 4

Preheat the oven to 300°F. Roughly chop up 4 cups of chicken to store in the fridge and reserve for later in the week. Heat the remaining chicken, uncovered, in an oven-safe baking dish for 35 minutes or so, until warmed through. Heat the sweet potatoes and zucchini, uncovered, in oven-safe storage containers in the same preheated oven for 25 to 30 minutes, until warm. Serve together.

RALLY INGREDIENTS

BBQ-Rubbed Chicken (page 32; reserve 4 cups diced chicken for egg rolls)

½ recipe Chili-Spiced Sweet Potatoes (page 33)

½ recipe Roasted Zucchini (page 35)

RALLY REMEDIES

- Serve spice-roasted tofu instead of chicken for a vegetarian option. You can even serve it like a stir-fry, with the sweet potatoes and zucchini mixed in.

- Offer ketchup for the kids to dunk away!

Squash-Lentil Soup *with* Crispy Curried Chickpeas, *and* Broccoli

SERVES 4 TO 6

RALLY INGREDIENTS

Squash-Lentil Soup (page 33)

Roasted Broccoli (page 35; reserve 6 cups for egg rolls)

Crispy Curried Chickpeas (page 34), saving some extras to top Santa Fe Bowls (page 44)

ADDITIONAL INGREDIENTS

1 cup Greek yogurt

1 lemon (optional)

Fresh loaf of bread (or garlic bread)

1 Preheat oven to 300°F. In a large stockpot, heat the soup over medium-low heat until warmed through. Add additional water as needed if it's too thick.

2 Roughly chop and store 6 cups of broccoli in the fridge for the egg rolls later in the week. Heat the remaining broccoli in the oven, uncovered, in an oven-safe storage container for about 20 minutes, until warmed through.

3 Ladle the soup into bowls. Top each bowl with a dollop of yogurt, some of the crispy chickpeas, and extra lemon zest and juice, if desired. Serve with bread for dunking and the broccoli as a side dish.

RALLY REMEDIES

- For pickier kids, blend the soup completely and serve with fun-shaped noodles mixed in.

- Serve with grilled cheese instead of the crispy chickpeas to appeal to younger ones. Or serve croutons or garlic bread instead.

Chicken-Broccoli Egg Rolls *with* Ranch Dip *and* Roasted Zucchini

SERVES 4 (MAKES 12 EGG ROLLS)

1 Preheat the oven to 425°F. Line a standard baking sheet with parchment paper and grease the parchment with cooking oil spray.

2 Make the egg rolls: In a medium bowl, mix together the chicken, broccoli, and BBQ sauce. Place one egg roll wrapper on a work surface and set a small cup or bowl of water nearby. Fill the egg roll wrapper with roughly ¼ cup of the chicken mixture. Fold the bottom up, then fold in the left and right sides and roll up the wrapper to enclose the filling. Dab some water on the edge to seal and place the egg roll seam side down on the prepared baking sheet. Repeat to make 12 egg rolls total.

3 Spray the egg rolls with cooking oil spray (or use a pastry brush to brush them with olive oil) and bake for 30 minutes or so, until golden brown and crisp. Transfer to a serving platter and cover to keep warm.

4 Meanwhile, spread the zucchini onto another parchment-lined baking sheet and warm in the oven, uncovered, for about 20 minutes, in the oven with the egg rolls.

5 Serve the egg rolls with the ranch dip and zucchini on the side.

RALLY INGREDIENTS

FOR THE EGG ROLLS

4 cups chopped BBQ-Rubbed Chicken (page 32)

6 cups chopped Roasted Broccoli (page 35)

FOR SERVING

½ recipe Roasted Zucchini (page 35)

½ recipe Ranch Dip (page 36)

ADDITIONAL INGREDIENTS

FOR THE EGG ROLLS

½ cup store-bought BBQ sauce

12 egg roll wrappers

Cooking oil spray or light olive oil

RALLY REMEDIES

- Get the kids involved in the egg roll rolling process. It's fun!

- If you're making these egg rolls vegetarian, stuff them with store-bought prepared tofu and/or your favorite sautéed vegetables.

- Lighten it up by stuffing the egg roll filling into tortillas, or make it gluten-free by serving the filling in lettuce cups.

Santa Fe Bowls

SERVES 4

RALLY INGREDIENTS

Basic Quinoa (page 36)

½ recipe Chili-Spiced Sweet Potatoes (page 33)

½ recipe Ranch Dip (page 36)

ADDITIONAL INGREDIENTS

1 (15.5-ounce) can black beans, drained and rinsed

1 (15.5-ounce) can corn kernels, drained

2 heads Bibb lettuce, coarsely chopped

1 pint cherry tomatoes, halved

Any leftover Crispy Curried Chickpeas (page 34), for topping

4 large eggs, hard- or soft-boiled (see page 266 for instructions on how to make a 7-minute egg)

Divvy up the quinoa, sweet potatoes, beans, corn, lettuce, tomatoes, chickpeas, and eggs among four bowls. Serve topped with the ranch.

RALLY REMEDIES

- When making salads for the family, section out the components so everyone can build their own. There's nothing worse than your kid refusing to eat the salad because the avocado is touching everything else when they didn't want avocado in their salad to begin with. Trust me on this one!

- Let the kids make tacos with the salad ingredients, or make breakfast burritos by scrambling the eggs instead of boiling and rolling the scrambled eggs in tortillas with the sweet potatoes, beans, corn, lettuce, and tomatoes.

GREEN
TAHINI

CHAPTER 2

Pesto *the* Besto

MAKES: 4 DINNERS, FOR 4 PEOPLE

If you couldn't tell by now, I'm all about the double-duty recipes. In this menu, you'll be prepping broccoli and broccoli pesto all at once to use in two different ways throughout the week. I also threw in some Middle Eastern flavors because they remind me of my childhood in Israel. My family lived there when I was in kindergarten through sixth grade, and while I love my friends and family there, it's the food that made a long-lasting impression on me. I always joke how I have the worst memory and can't remember what my friends and I used to play as kids, but I vividly remember what their mom would cook for us during the playdate. It's bizarre! Food, apparently, has always played a role in my life.

- **Broccoli Pesto Baked Halibut** *with* **Roasted Broccoli** *and* **Smashed Lemony Potatoes**

- **Shawarma Chicken Pita Pockets** *with* **Honey-Roasted Carrots**

- **Baked Shakshuka** *with* **Green Tahini**

- **Loaded Baked Potato Bar** *with* **Broccoli Pesto**

PREP

1 **Baked Potatoes**

2 **Roasted Broccoli** *and* **Broccoli Pesto**

3 **Honey-Roasted Carrots**

4 **Shakshuka Sauce**

5 **Shawarma Chicken**

6 **Green Tahini**

7 **Broccoli Pesto Baked Halibut**

NOTES & SWAPS

PREP SMART

- Buy baby carrots to save time on peeling.
- Pine nuts tend to be pricey! Feel free to swap them out for cashews or sunflower seeds when making the pesto.
- Mix some heavy cream into the shakshuka to turn it into a rosa sauce and give it an even richer flavor.

PREP IT MORE KID-FRIENDLY

- Serve the broccoli pesto with tortellini or gnocchi instead of stuffed baked potatoes for Thursday's dinner. Just bake 3 potatoes for the Smashed Lemony Potatoes on Tuesday if you're going that route. Buy frozen gnocchi or tortellini, cook according to the package directions, and toss in the pesto.
- Sprinkle some shredded cheese over the smashed potatoes in the last 5 minutes of roasting. Kids love these!
- Have a hard time getting your kids to eat fish and want to nix the halibut? Instead of coating the fish with the pesto, use some of the pesto to make flavorful scrambled eggs or spread it over a flatbread and make Pesto and Egg Flowers (page 271). You can also make broccoli pesto quesadillas with smashed black beans for more protein.
- If you don't like shakshuka with the traditional eggs, simmer 4 fillets of fish in the shakshuka sauce for a Moroccan-style dish. Throw in some spicy peppers for good measure, and drizzle with the tahini.

PREP IT GLUTEN-FREE/LIGHTEN IT UP

- Instead of shawarma pita pockets, you can make shawarma bowls by loading all your favorite veggies in a bowl and topping them with the chicken, carrots, and green tahini (loosen it with water to achieve a dressing consistency).
- Instead of loaded potatoes, prepare a spaghetti squash and mix in the pesto with extra shredded mozzarella for a lower-carb option! It's also great mixed into cauliflower rice.

PREP IT VEGETARIAN

- Instead of fish, use the broccoli pesto as a sauce for pasta, gnocchi, tortellini, or pizza!
- Replace the chicken in the shawarma with cauliflower; just load the cauliflower with the shawarma spices and roast.

COOKING TOOLS AND EQUIPMENT NEEDED

- Chef's knife
- Cutting board
- Aluminum foil
- 1 extra-large baking sheet and 1 standard baking sheet, or 3 standard baking sheets
- 16-ounce wide-mouthed storage jar with lid
- 32-ounce wide-mouthed storage jar with lid
- Immersion blender, high-speed blender, or food processor
- 10-inch oven-safe skillet
- Resealable bag
- Microplane
- Vegetable peeler
- 9 x 13-inch baking dish

GROCERY LIST

PRODUCE

- 8 medium russet potatoes **1**
- 45 ounces broccoli florets, or 5 heads broccoli **2**
- 6 garlic cloves **2** **4** **6**
- 1 bunch basil **2**
- 12 large carrots **3**
- 1 onion **4**
- 2 red bell peppers **4**
- 3 lemons **4** **6** + 4 for R
- 1 bunch parsley **4** **6**
- 2 English cucumbers R
- 4 medium tomatoes R
- 1 bunch scallions R

PANTRY

- Light olive oil
- Extra-virgin olive oil
- Kosher salt
- Pepper
- ¼ cup pine nuts **2**
- 2 tablespoons honey **3**
- 3½ teaspoons garlic powder **3** **4** **5**
- ½ teaspoon ground sumac **3**
- 1 tablespoon plus 1½ teaspoons sweet paprika **3** **4** **5**
- 1 teaspoon ground cumin **4**
- 1 teaspoon ground coriander **5**
- 1 teaspoon ground turmeric **5**
- ¼ teaspoon ground cinnamon **5**
- ⅓ cup tahini **6**
- 1 (28-ounce) can crushed tomatoes (I love Don Pepino pizza sauce here) **4**
- 1 (15-ounce) can black olives R
- 1 (15 ounce) can black beans R
- ½ cup chopped sun-dried tomatoes packed in oil R

- 4 pitas R
- Bread (optional) R

DAIRY

- ¼ cup grated Parmesan cheese **2**
- 3 cups shredded cheddar or mozzarella cheese R
- 2 cups sour cream R

PROTEIN

- 2 pounds boneless, skinless chicken breasts or thighs **5**
- 4 (8-ounce) skin-on halibut fillets (you can use flounder, cod, or striped bass here as well) **7**
- 8 large eggs R

*The "**R**" symbolizes ingredients you'll be using to Rally throughout the week—these won't be needed in the Sunday prep!

PREP

Time to prep! Set aside about an hour on
your Prep day to make these recipes,
then store them to use for Rally meals
during the week.

1 Baked Potatoes

SERVES 8

8 medium russet potatoes,
  scrubbed

1 Preheat the oven to 425°F.

2 Prick the potatoes carefully with a knife and wrap each one individually in aluminum foil. Place the potatoes directly on the bottom oven rack and bake for 45 to 50 minutes. Unwrap and allow to cool completely, then store in a covered container or storage bag in the fridge.

2 Roasted Broccoli *and* Broccoli Pesto

MAKES 8 SERVINGS ROASTED BROCCOLI AND 3 CUPS PESTO

FOR THE ROASTED BROCCOLI

45 ounces broccoli florets, or
  5 heads broccoli

4 to 5 tablespoons light olive oil

Kosher salt and pepper

FOR THE BROCCOLI PESTO

1 garlic clove, peeled

¼ cup packed fresh basil (tough
  stems discarded)

¼ cup pine nuts (or other nuts/
  seeds such as sunflower
  seeds, cashews, or walnuts)

¼ cup grated Parmesan cheese

½ teaspoon kosher salt

⅛ teaspoon pepper

½ cup light olive oil

1 Make the roasted broccoli: Preheat the oven to 425°F. Line one extra-large baking sheet or two standard baking sheets with parchment paper. Spread the broccoli over the prepared pan(s) and drizzle with the oil. Season with salt and pepper and massage to coat. Roast on the center rack for 30 to 35 minutes. Reserve 2 cups for the broccoli pesto and store the remainder, covered, in the fridge.

2 Make the broccoli pesto: Place the reserved roasted broccoli in a wide-mouthed storage jar large enough to fit the head of an immersion blender. Add the garlic, basil, pine nuts, Parmesan, salt, pepper, and olive oil and blend until smooth. (Alternatively, combine the ingredients in a high-speed blender or food processor and blend until smooth.) If the pesto seems too thick, drizzle in some more olive oil and blend again. Cover and store in the fridge.

HOT TIPS

- If you're cutting up your own broccoli, cut the crowns into medium florets and cut up some of the tender stem parts so as not to waste them—they're great blended up in the pesto. Discard any of the tough or fibrous stems. Alternatively, use precut florets for ease.

- While the broccoli is roasting, start prepping the Honey-Roasted Carrots and then come back to assemble the pesto!

- Precut vegetables such as broccoli, brussels sprouts, butternut squash, and cauliflower are major time savers and allow you to enjoy homemade food with a fraction of the effort. Worth every penny, in my opinion.

3 Honey-Roasted Carrots

SERVES 6

12 large carrots, peeled and cut on an angle into ½-inch thin slices

2 tablespoons honey

3 to 4 tablespoons light olive oil

½ teaspoon sweet paprika

½ teaspoon garlic powder

½ teaspoon ground sumac

Kosher salt and pepper

Preheat the oven to 425°F. Line a standard baking sheet with parchment paper. Spread the carrots over the baking sheet and coat in the honey and oil. Sprinkle with the paprika, garlic powder, and sumac and season with salt and pepper. Roast for about 35 minutes, until tender. Let cool, then store, covered, in the fridge.

HOT TIP

• No sumac? You can always skip it, or use some lemon zest instead.

4 Shakshuka Sauce

MAKES SAUCE FOR 4 TO 6 SERVINGS

1 tablespoon light olive oil

1 onion, finely diced

2 red bell peppers, finely diced (2 cups)

4 garlic cloves, minced

1 teaspoon garlic powder

1 teaspoon sweet paprika

1 teaspoon ground cumin

½ teaspoon kosher salt

1 (28-ounce) can crushed tomatoes

Zest and juice of 1 large lemon

¼ cup fresh parsley, coarsely chopped

In a large oven-safe skillet, heat the oil over medium-high heat. Add the onion, bell peppers, and garlic and cook, stirring, until softened, about 10 minutes. Add the garlic powder, paprika, cumin, salt, tomatoes, lemon zest and juice, and parsley. Cover and cook over medium-low heat for 15 to 20 minutes, until thickened. Let cool, then store, covered, in the same pan, or transfer to a 9 x 13-inch pan, cover, and store.

HOT TIP

• If you're making shakshuka as a stand-alone recipe, head to page 63 for cooking directions.

Shawarma Chicken

SERVES 6

Place the oil, paprika, garlic powder, salt, turmeric, coriander, and cinnamon in a resealable bag and massage to combine. Add the chicken and seal the bag. Massage again to coat the chicken in the mixture and store in the fridge.

HOT TIPS

- If you're making this vegetarian, simply replace the chicken with cauliflower florets or even seitan.

- If you're making this as a stand-alone recipe, head to page 60 for cooking instructions.

3 tablespoons light olive oil

1 tablespoon sweet paprika

2 teaspoons garlic powder

2 teaspoons kosher salt

1 teaspoon ground turmeric

1 teaspoon ground coriander

¼ teaspoon ground cinnamon

2 pounds boneless, skinless chicken breast or thighs, cut into ½ inch strips

 # Green Tahini

MAKES 1½ CUPS

Combine the tahini, parsley, lemon zest and juice, garlic, and water in a tall storage container and season with salt and pepper. Use an immersion blender to blend until smooth. (Alternatively, you can use a high-speed blender or food processor.) Keep adding water in small amounts until you've reached the desired consistency. Season with additional salt as needed, cover, and store in the fridge.

⅓ cup tahini

½ cup fresh parsley leaves, roughly torn

Zest and juice of 2 lemons

1 large garlic clove

½ cup water, plus more as needed

Kosher salt and pepper

7 Broccoli Pesto Baked Halibut

SERVES 4

Light olive oil for greasing

4 (8-ounce) skin-on halibut fillets, bones removed (you can use flounder, cod, or striped bass here as well)

Kosher salt and pepper

1 cup Broccoli Pesto (page 52)

Grease a 9 x 13-inch baking dish with oil. Pat the halibut dry with paper towels and place the fillets in the prepared baking dish, flesh side up. Season the fish with salt and pepper and spread ¼ cup of the pesto over each fillet, creating a crust. Store, covered, in the fridge.

HOT TIP

• If you're making this as a stand-alone recipe, head to page 59 for cooking directions.

RALLY

Get ready to Rally! Time to take all those
Prep staples and use them to
create delicious meals for the week.

Broccoli Pesto Baked Halibut *with* Roasted Broccoli *and* Smashed Lemony Potatoes

SERVES 4

1 Preheat the oven to 450°F. Line a standard baking sheet with parchment paper.

2 Remove the halibut from the fridge and let it come to room temperature while you prep the potatoes.

3 Slice the potatoes into 1-inch-thick rounds and place them on the prepared baking sheet. Lightly smash them with your palm or the bottom of a measuring cup to thin them out and create more surface area for crispy edges. (Keep in mind that these are supposed to break apart and look rustic.) Drizzle with the oil and season liberally with salt and pepper. Roast for 35 minutes or so, until golden brown and crisp.

4 Bake the fish, uncovered, in the same oven for 20 to 30 minutes, until a crust has formed and the fish is easily flaked with a fork; the time will vary depending on the thickness of the fish, so start checking it at the 20-minute mark.

5 Place the broccoli onto a parchment-lined baking sheet and warm in the same oven for about 15 minutes.

6 Remove the potatoes from the oven and top with the lemon zest and juice. Serve the halibut with the potatoes and broccoli on the side.

RALLY INGREDIENTS

Uncooked Broccoli Pesto Baked Halibut (page 56)

3 Baked Potatoes (page 52)

½ recipe Roasted Broccoli (page 52)

ADDITIONAL INGREDIENTS

3 to 4 tablespoons light olive oil

Kosher salt and pepper

Zest and juice of 1 lemon

RALLY REMEDIES

• To make this vegetarian, swap out the fish for broccoli pesto quesadillas or Pesto and Egg Flowers (page 271). Alternatively, add diced baked potato and frozen peas to scrambled eggs. Top with pesto.

Shawarma Chicken Pita Pockets *with* Honey-Roasted Carrots

SERVES 4

RALLY INGREDIENTS

Uncooked Shawarma Chicken
(page 55)

Honey-Roasted Carrots
(page 54)

Green Tahini (page 55)

ADDITIONAL INGREDIENTS

Juice of 2 lemons

2 English cucumbers, finely
diced

4 medium tomatoes, finely diced

3 scallions, thinly sliced

Handful of fresh parsley, finely
chopped

Kosher salt and pepper

1 to 2 tablespoons extra-virgin
olive oil

1 to 2 tablespoons light olive oil,
plus more for greasing

4 store-bought pitas, for serving

1 Preheat the oven to 300°F.

2 Remove the chicken from the fridge and add half of the lemon juice. Seal the bag again and massage to coat. Set aside to come to room temperature for a few minutes.

3 Heat the carrots, uncovered, in an oven-safe storage container for 25 minutes or so, until warmed through.

4 In a medium bowl, combine the cucumbers, tomatoes, scallions and parsley. Add the remaining lemon juice, season with salt and pepper, and drizzle with 1 to 2 tablespoons of the extra-virgin olive oil. Toss to coat, then set the salad aside.

5 In a large heavy-bottomed skillet or grill pan, heat the 1 to 2 tablespoons light olive oil over medium-high heat. Using tongs, remove some chicken from the marinade, shake off as much marinade as possible, and place it in the pan. Fry on all sides until cooked through, 4 to 5 minutes, then transfer to a plate. Repeat with the remaining chicken, adding more oil to the pan as needed between batches; discarding any marinade remaining in the bag.

6 Serve the chicken in the pitas with the green tahini, roasted carrots, and salad. Reserve any leftover tahini and carrots for the Baked Shakshuka (page 63), if you like.

RALLY REMEDIES

- If you're swapping out the chicken for cauliflower or seitan, remove it from the marinade and roast on a parchment-lined baking sheet at 425°F for 25 to 35 minutes.

- Omit the pitas and make shawarma salad bowls.

- These are also fun served like fajitas in tortillas with lettuce, tomato, and lime.

Baked Shakshuka *with* Green Tahini

SERVES 4

1 Preheat the oven to 400°F.

2 Remove the shakshuka sauce from the fridge and uncover it. Make 8 wells, using the back of a spoon, in the sauce and crack an egg into each well.

3 If you're using up leftover carrots, place them on a baking sheet and heat them in the same oven for about 20 minutes to serve alongside shakshuka. (Alternatively, you can mix them into the shakshuka sauce prior to adding the eggs so it's a complete one-pan meal served family-style.)

4 Start checking the shakshuka at the 20-minute mark and continue cooking and checking often until the eggs have reached the desired doneness. To test, you can poke the eggs gently with a fork. Keep a close watch on them if you like them runnier.

5 Top the shakshuka with the leftover green tahini (if using), parsley, and lemon zest and juice. Serve with fresh bread, toasted in the same oven to warm through.

RALLY INGREDIENTS

Shakshuka Sauce (page 54)

Leftover Honey-Roasted Carrots (page 54; optional)

Leftover Green Tahini (page 55; optional)

ADDITIONAL INGREDIENTS

8 large eggs

Small bunch fresh parsley

Zest and juice of 1 lemon

Loaf of bread or pitas, for serving

RALLY REMEDIES

• You can of course cook the shakshuka on the stovetop for a more traditional preparation, but I love that the oven is hands-off and does the work for me. It also heats the carrots and toasts the bread or pitas all at once.

• Place 4 fish fillets into the shakshuka sauce and roast at 400°F for 25 to 35 minutes or simmer on the stovetop over medium heat for 15 minutes for a whole new dish.

• Make this vegan by throwing in some canned chickpeas and the Honey-Roasted Carrots and serve with bread. You can also mix any leftover roasted vegetables you have in the fridge into the shakshuka sauce to make it an even more complete meal.

Loaded Baked Potato Bar *with* Broccoli Pesto

SERVES 4 OR 5

RALLY INGREDIENTS

5 Baked Potatoes (page 52)

2 cups Broccoli Pesto (page 52)

Leftover Roasted Broccoli (page 52; optional)

TOPPINGS

3 cups shredded cheddar or mozzarella cheese

2 cups sour cream

4 scallions, thinly sliced

1 (15-ounce) can olives, drained

1 (15-ounce) can black beans, drained and rinsed

½ cup chopped sun-dried tomatoes packed in oil

Optional leftover fresh basil and/or parsley from your Prep

1 Preheat the oven to 300°F. Heat the potatoes in an oven-safe storage container or baking sheet until warmed through.

2 Place each topping, including the pesto and broccoli, in its own little bowl. Once warm, cut each potato in half lengthwise and serve them on a fun board, with all the toppings alongside so everyone can assemble their own.

RALLY REMEDIES

- To serve this differently, cube the baked potatoes and place on a baking sheet. Sprinkle your toppings of choice all over the top and bake in a 400°F oven until the cheese is bubbling and golden. Serve family-style, like nachos!

- Mix the pesto into cauliflower rice, gluten-free pasta, or spaghetti squash to replace the potato.

- Make a batch of tortellini or gnocchi and mix in the pesto instead of serving it with the potatoes.

CHAPTER 3

Brekkie *for* Din

MAKES: 4 DINNERS, FOR 4 PEOPLE

Who doesn't like breakfast for dinner? My kids ask me for it all the time, as it's a fun change to the typical dinner routine. You're going to love this unique spin on french toast. We're making cornbread to serve with the picadillo and using the rest as our "bread" for the french toast. Oh, and start giving your food superhero names. Your kids will come running!

- Spatchcocked Chicken *with* Roots *and* Hulk Soup

- Beef Picadillo *with* Cornbread *and* Soy Brussels Sprouts

- Green Goddess Wedge Chicken Salad

- Cornbread French Toast *with* Eggs *and* Pickled Vegetables

PREP

1. Spatchcocked Chicken *with* Roots

2. Hulk Soup

3. Cornbread

4. Beef Picadillo

5. Soy Brussels Sprouts

6. Pickled Vegetables

7. Green Goddess Sauce

8. Egg Mixture *for* French Toast

NOTES & SWAPS

PREP SMART

- Mince all the garlic in advance or buy peeled or minced garlic. It will save lots of time this week.
- Buy pre-spatchcocked chickens, or roast whole chickens and increase the cooking time.
- Buy cleaned and halved Brussels sprouts to save time. Trust me!
- If you can't get a ripe avocado, simply replace it with ½ cup good-quality mayonnaise.
- Swap out quinoa for any other grain you prefer to eat with the chicken.
- We've got lots of herbs in this week's menu. Wash them all before you prep.

PREP IT MORE KID-FRIENDLY

- Instead of wedge salad, make chicken sandwiches, serving the shredded chicken in baguettes with Green Goddess Sauce.
- Serve the picadillo in buns and call it sloppy Joes for a more familiar meal, or serve it in taco shells!

PREP IT GLUTEN-FREE/LIGHTEN IT UP

- Nix the cornbread recipe and instead buy gluten-free or lower-carb sliced bread. Use that to make the french toast. Alternatively, make the cornbread with gluten-free flour.
- Use gluten-free bread for the bread crumbs on the wedge salad, or omit the bread crumbs altogether and serve the chicken with Green Goddess Sauce in Bibb lettuce cups.

PREP IT VEGETARIAN

- Use Beyond Beef to make the picadillo.
- Instead of the chicken, buy 3 (16-ounce) blocks of tofu to roast.

COOKING TOOLS AND EQUIPMENT NEEDED

- Chef's knife
- Cutting board
- 1 extra-large baking sheet or 2 standard baking sheets
- 2 large (6- to 8-quart) stockpots
- Microplane
- Large (10-inch) skillet
- 2 (32-ounce) storage jars with tight-fitting lids
- Immersion blender or food processor
- 9 x 13-inch baking dish
- Medium (3-quart) saucepan
- Meat thermometer
- Medium bowl
- Vegetable peeler
- 24-ounce storage bowl with lid

GROCERY LIST

PRODUCE

- 2 red onions **1**
- 4 large parsnips **1**
- 2 onions **2** **4**
- 2 cups baby carrots **6**
- 1 green bell pepper **4**
- 10 garlic cloves **2** **4** **5** **6** **7**
- 6 medium zucchini **2**
- 6 ounces baby spinach **2**
- 1 big bunch parsley **7**
- 1 big bunch basil **7**
- 24 ounces bagged halved prewashed medium Brussels sprouts (or 2 pounds loose) **5**
- 1 big bunch dill **2** **6** **7**
- 3 Persian cucumbers **6**
- 5 medium lemons **1** **2** **7**
- 1 ripe medium avocado **7**
- 1 large head iceberg lettuce **R**

PANTRY

- Light olive oil
- Extra-virgin olive oil
- Kosher salt
- Pepper
- 2 teaspoons garlic powder **1**
- 2 teaspoons onion powder **1**
- 1 teaspoon dried rosemary **1**
- 3 teaspoons dried oregano **1** **4**
- 1 teaspoon ground cumin **4**
- 1 teaspoon mild chili powder **8**
- 3 tablespoons low-sodium soy sauce **5**
- ¼ teaspoon red chile flakes **5** (optional)
- 1 cup plus 3 tablespoons rice vinegar **6** **7**
- 1 (28-ounce) can crushed tomatoes **4**
- 2 tablespoons tomato paste **4**
- 1 tablespoon capers **4**

- ¼ cup pimiento-stuffed olives or sliced olives of choice **4**
- 1 cup pure maple syrup **3** **5** **6** **8**
- 1½ cups fine cornmeal **3**
- 1½ cups all-purpose flour **3**
- 1 tablespoon baking powder **3**
- ½ teaspoon baking soda **3**
- 32 ounces (4 cups) vegetable stock **2**
- 1½ cups plain soy milk or almond milk **3**
- ½ sourdough baguette (6 to 8 ounces) **R**

DAIRY

- ½ cup milk or nondairy alternative **8**
- 2 to 3 tablespoons unsalted butter **R**

PROTEIN

- 2 (5- to 6-pound) whole chickens, spatchcocked or butterflied **1**
- 1½ pounds ground beef **4**
- 6 large eggs **3** **8** + 4 for R

> *The "R" symbolizes ingredients you'll be using to Rally throughout the week—these won't be needed in the Sunday prep!

PREP

Time to prep! Set aside about an hour on your Prep day to make these recipes, then store them to use for Rally meals during the week.

1 Spatchcocked Chicken *with* Roots

SERVES 8

2 (5- to 6-pound) whole
   chickens, spatchcocked or
   butterflied

2 red onions, halved and cut into
   16 wedges

4 large parsnips, peeled and cut
   on an angle into ½-inch-thick
   pieces

Kosher salt and pepper

2 teaspoons dried oregano

2 teaspoons garlic powder

2 teaspoons onion powder

1 teaspoon dried rosemary

2 lemons, halved

5 to 6 tablespoons light olive oil

1 Preheat the oven to 400°F. Line an extra-large baking sheet or two standard baking sheets with parchment paper.

2 Place the chickens on the prepared baking sheet(s) and pat them dry with a paper towel to achieve crispier and more golden skin. Divvy up the onions and parsnips and scatter them around the chickens. Season both chickens thoroughly with salt and pepper on both sides, seasoning the vegetables as well. Season the chicken and vegetables with the oregano, garlic powder, onion powder, and rosemary, then squeeze the juice from the lemon halves all over. Place the squeezed lemon halves on the baking sheet (tuck some under the chicken too) to cook along with the chicken. Drizzle everything with the oil and massage to coat both sides of the chickens. Rub some of the seasoning under the skin as well to create a more flavorful chicken.

3 Roast, uncovered, ideally on the top rack to encourage extra browning, for 50 to 60 minutes, until the chickens are cooked through and have reached an internal temperature of 165°F. Let cool and squeeze extra lemon juice from the cooked lemon halves all over and discard the rest. Store the chickens and vegetables, covered, in the fridge.

HOT TIPS

• You can make this with whole chickens, if preferred. Simply increase the cooking time to 75 to 80 minutes, or until the internal temperature reaches 165°F.

• Want to spatchcock your own chicken? It's really easy and kind of fun! Place your whole chicken breast side down on a cutting board. Starting by the thigh, cut along one side of the backbone with kitchen shears (ideally) or a serrated knife. Rotate the chicken and cut the other side of the backbone until it can be removed. Flip the chicken so it's breast side up and press the chicken down at the center (kind of like CPR) to further splay it open. Preparing the chicken like this allows for much faster cooking and a seriously crisp exterior!

• To make this meal vegetarian, cut 3 (16-ounce) blocks of tofu into ½-inch-thick steaks and dry off well. Cook just as you would the chickens, decreasing cook time as needed.

2 Hulk Soup

SERVES 6 TO 8

In a large stockpot, heat the oil over high heat. Add the onion and garlic and cook until softened, 4 to 5 minutes. Add the zucchini, spinach, stock, and dill, salt and pepper to season, and bring to a boil. Reduce the heat to maintain a simmer, cover, and cook for 15 minutes, or until the zucchini is tender. Add the lemon zest and juice and blend with an immersion blender until smooth. Season with additional salt and pepper as needed. Let cool and store in the fridge in the pot to easily heat up later in the week.

2 tablespoons light olive oil

1 onion, diced

3 garlic cloves, coarsely chopped

6 medium zucchini, coarsely chopped

6 ounces baby spinach

4 cups (32 ounces) vegetable stock

½ cup fresh dill, coarsely chopped

Kosher salt and pepper

Zest and juice of 1 lemon

HOT TIP

• Use up any leftover fresh herbs from this week's Prep by blending them into the soup. The more, the merrier!

3 Cornbread

SERVES 8

Cooking oil spray or light olive oil, for greasing

2 large eggs

1½ cups plain soy milk or almond milk

⅓ cup pure maple syrup

½ cup light olive oil or other neutral cooking oil, plus more for greasing the baking dish

1½ cups fine cornmeal

1½ cups all-purpose flour

1 tablespoon baking powder

½ teaspoon baking soda

1¼ teaspoons kosher salt

1 Preheat the oven to 400°F. Grease a 9 x 13-inch baking dish with oil.

2 In a medium bowl, whisk together the eggs, milk of choice, maple syrup, and oil. Add the cornmeal, flour, baking powder, baking soda, and salt and mix until smooth. Pour the batter into the prepared baking dish and bake until golden brown, about 20 minutes. Let cool, then store, covered, in the fridge.

HOT TIPS

- Storing the cornbread in the fridge will ensure it stays fresh for Thursday's french toast. It also freezes beautifully.

- I love turning this cornbread into dessert or breakfast. Mix in ½ cup granulated sugar, a dash of cinnamon, and top with 1 cup fresh strawberries, cherries, or blueberries before baking. Bake according to recipe directions.

- Use a cup-for-cup gluten-free flour to replace the all-purpose flour, if needed.

4 Beef Picadillo

SERVES 4

1 In a medium stockpot, heat the oil over medium-high heat. Add the bell pepper, onion, and garlic and cook until softened. Add the beef and season with the salt, oregano, and cumin. Cook, breaking up the meat using a spatula, until nicely browned.

2 Add the crushed tomatoes, tomato paste, capers, and olives. Bring to a boil, then reduce the heat to maintain a simmer, cover, and cook for 15 minutes. Remove from the heat. Let cool, then store, covered, in the fridge.

2 to 3 tablespoons light olive oil

1 green bell pepper, cut into small dice

1 onion, finely diced

3 garlic cloves, minced

1½ pounds ground beef

1 teaspoon kosher salt

1 teaspoon dried oregano

1 teaspoon ground cumin

1 (28-ounce) can crushed tomatoes

2 tablespoons tomato paste

1 tablespoon capers, coarsely chopped

¼ cup pimiento-stuffed olives, coarsely chopped

HOT TIPS

• Use Beyond Beef to make this vegetarian.

• If your family is anti olives, leave them out!

5 Soy Brussels Sprouts

SERVES 8

24 ounces bagged halved washed medium Brussels sprouts (or 2 pounds loose)

¼ cup light olive oil

Kosher salt and pepper

2 garlic cloves, minced

2 tablespoons pure maple syrup

3 tablespoons low-sodium soy sauce

Kosher salt and pepper

¼ teaspoon red chile flakes (optional)

1 Trim and halve your Brussels sprouts if they aren't already. If there are some larger ones in the bunch cut them in quarters to ensure the sprouts all cook through at the same time. In a large skillet, heat 2 tablespoons of the oil over high heat. Add the Brussels sprouts and season with salt and black pepper. Fry until charred in some places, about 5 minutes. Drizzle in 2 tablespoons more oil and give the sprouts a stir. Reduce the heat to medium, cover with a lid, and cook for 5 minutes, or until cooked through the center.

2 Uncover and add the garlic, maple syrup, and soy sauce. Raise the heat back to medium-high and cook, uncovered, stirring every so often to coat everything in the sticky sauce, for 6 to 8 minutes more. Season with additional salt and pepper as needed and add chile flakes (if using). Let cool, then store, covered, in the fridge.

HOT TIPS

- I love giving the same treatment to shishito peppers and green beans!

- If you have space in the oven and want to roast these, you can combine all the ingredients on a baking sheet and roast at 400°F for 40 to 45 minutes or so, until the sauce has become sticky and the Brussels sprouts are tender.

6 Pickled Vegetables

MAKES 4 CUPS

Put the garlic, dill, cucumbers, and carrots in a large storage jar with a tight-fitting lid. In a small saucepan, combine the vinegar, water, maple syrup, and salt. Bring just to a boil over high heat and then pour over the vegetables. Swirl around slightly to coat the vegetables in the pickling liquid. Don't worry if the vegetables aren't all submerged into the liquid right away, as they will be once they pickle for a few hours. Let cool completely, then cover and store in the fridge.

1 garlic clove, peeled and cut in half

¼ cup fresh dill

3 Persian cucumbers, cut into ¼-inch-thick rounds (2 cups)

2 cups sliced baby carrots (¼-inch-thick rounds)

1 cup rice vinegar

¼ cup water

¼ cup pure maple syrup

2 teaspoons kosher salt

HOT TIP

• I love a good punch of acid in all my food, and that's easy to achieve when you have a bunch of pickles prepped and ready to go. Use up any vegetables you have lying around in the vegetable bin. I love making the same recipe with cauliflower, radishes, and jalapeño. Replace the dill with a bay leaf and add a sprinkle of oregano to give these a whole new flavor!

• If you have store-bought pickles at home, save the brine and keep adding new vegetables so that you always have new pickles ready to go. They're best after they've had a few days to sit in the liquid.

7 Green Goddess Sauce

MAKES ABOUT 1½ CUPS

1 cup fresh parsley, roughly torn

½ cup fresh dill, roughly torn

½ cup fresh basil, roughly torn

1 ripe medium avocado

Juice of 2 medium lemons
(about 6 tablespoons)

3 tablespoons rice vinegar

1 garlic clove, peeled

¼ cup plus 2 tablespoons
extra-virgin olive oil

Kosher salt and pepper

Combine the parsley, dill, basil, avocado, lemon juice, vinegar, garlic, and oil in a wide-mouthed storage jar large enough to fit the head of an immersion blender and pulse to blend until smooth. Add a few splashes of water to thin the sauce if it gets too thick. Season with salt and pepper. Cover and store in the fridge.

HOT TIPS

- You can also prep this sauce in a food processor or blender, but an immersion blender is fastest and requires the least cleanup of the three options.

- Can't find a ripe avocado? Use ½ cup mayonnaise instead. You can also sub in Greek yogurt or sour cream for a slightly tangier sauce. They're all addicting!

8 Egg Mixture *for* French Toast

MAKES MIXTURE FOR 8 PIECES OF FRENCH TOAST

4 large eggs

½ cup milk or nondairy
alternative

¼ cup pure maple syrup

1 teaspoon mild chili powder

¼ teaspoon kosher salt

Whisk together all the ingredients in a medium storage bowl. Cover and store in the fridge.

HOT TIPS

- For a faster Prep day, nix the Egg Mixture for French Toast and make it later in the week!

- If you're making this as a stand-alone recipe, make a batch of cornbread (see page 74) and then head to page 87 for cooking directions.

RALLY

Get ready to Rally! Time to take all those
Prep staples and use them to
create delicious meals for the week.

Spatchcocked Chicken *with* Roots *and* Hulk Soup

SERVES 4

RALLY INGREDIENTS

1 Spatchcocked Chicken with Roots and all vegetables (page 72)

Hulk Soup (page 73)

¼ cup Green Goddess Sauce (page 78), for topping soup (optional)

ADDITIONAL INGREDIENTS

Extra-virgin olive oil, for drizzling

1 Preheat the oven to 300°F. Heat the chicken and vegetables on a baking sheet or in an oven-safe storage container, uncovered, for 30 to 35 minutes, or until heated through.

2 Meanwhile, in a saucepan, heat the soup, covered, over medium heat until warm.

3 Serve the soup topped with a dollop of Green Goddess Sauce, if desired, and a drizzle of extra-virgin olive oil. Serve the chicken and vegetables for the main course.

RALLY REMEDIES

- Serve roasted tofu to make this meal vegetarian (see Hot Tip, page 72).

- Make chicken more fun for kids to eat by wrapping the drumsticks with napkins and calling them "chickie pops"— sounds wacky, but my kids love it!

Beef Picadillo *with* Cornbread *and* Soy Brussels Sprouts

SERVES 4

1 Preheat the oven to 300°F.

2 Heat the beef picadillo, covered, in an oven-safe storage container for 30 minutes, or until warmed through.

3 Heat the Brussels sprouts, uncovered, in the same oven, in an oven-safe storage container for 15 to 20 minutes, until warm.

4 Line a baking sheet with parchment paper. Remove the cornbread from the fridge and cut it in half. Transfer half the cornbread to the baking sheet. Tightly wrap the other half in plastic wrap and return it to the fridge for use later in the week.

5 Heat the cornbread in the same preheated oven for about 10 minutes right before serving. Cut the cornbread into squares and serve the picadillo with the cornbread and Brussels sprouts on the side.

RALLY INGREDIENTS

Beef Picadillo (page 75)

Soy Brussels Sprouts (page 76)

½ recipe Cornbread (page 74)

RALLY REMEDY

- Serve the picadillo on buns to make sloppy Joes. If all else fails, mix some marinara into it and call it a meat sauce if your kids put up a fight!

Green Goddess Wedge Chicken Salad

RALLY INGREDIENTS

Chicken (half or all remaining from page 72), cubed or shredded

Remaining Green Goddess Sauce (page 78)

½ recipe Pickled Vegetables (page 77)

ADDITIONAL INGREDIENTS

1 large head iceberg lettuce

3 to 4 tablespoons light olive oil

Sourdough baguette (6 to 8 ounces), torn into ½-inch pieces

Kosher salt and pepper

1 Discard any wilted outer leaves from the lettuce and cut the head into quarters, cutting through the root so the wedges stay intact. Place the quarters in one section of a serving platter.

2 In a large skillet, heat the oil over high heat. Add the torn bread, season with salt and pepper, and stir to coat the bread in the oil. Let the bread crisp up and fry on all sides until deeply golden brown like croutons, 4 to 5 minutes. Place the croutons on another section of the serving platter.

3 Add another tablespoon of oil to the same skillet and warm the chicken over medium heat for 5 to 6 minutes. Add the chicken to the platter.

4 Place the Green Goddess sauce in a little bowl with a spoon on the platter as well. Let everyone build their own wedge salad, starting with the lettuce and topping it with the chicken, croutons, and sauce. Serve with the pickled vegetables as an extra salad topper.

RALLY REMEDIES

- This salad is also great with cold chicken, and it's delicious chopped up as a more traditional salad in a bowl as well.

- Switch it up by making chicken sandwiches, serving the Green Goddess Sauce and chicken in a baguette. Alternatively, use tofu or seitan to make this vegetarian.

- Use gluten-free bread for the croutons if needed.

Cornbread French Toast *with* Eggs *and* Pickled Vegetables

SERVES 4

1 Cut the cornbread into 4 even squares and transfer them to a cutting board. Gently split each square through its center to create two thinner squares resembling slices of bread. These thin slices give you loads of surface area for delicious crispy edges.

2 In a large nonstick skillet, melt 1 tablespoon of the butter over medium heat. Working with 3 squares at a time, dunk each square into the Egg Mixture for French Toast, letting it soak for a few seconds on each side, then shake off any excess egg mixture and place the bread in the pan. Fry for 3 to 4 minutes per side, until golden and cooked through. Transfer to a plate, add more butter to the pan as needed, and repeat with the remaining squares.

3 Fry the eggs according to your preference. Serve the french toast topped with fried eggs and the pickled vegetables on the side.

RALLY INGREDIENTS

½ recipe Cornbread
(page 74)

Egg Mixture for French Toast
(page 78)

½ recipe Pickled Vegetables
(page 77)

ADDITIONAL INGREDIENTS

2 to 3 tablespoons unsalted butter, plus more as needed

4 large eggs

RALLY REMEDIES

• This french toast is super fun to serve with fried chicken as a Southern meal!

• Use gluten-free bread instead of the cornbread, if necessary.

• Scramble the eggs for those who don't like fried eggs.

CHAPTER 4

Do That Hokey Poke

MAKES: 4 DINNERS FOR 4 PEOPLE

Poke bowls have become our favorite dinner that usually becomes school lunches the next day. Andi and Jolie make mini poke tacos by stuffing rice and veggies (sometimes cooked fish too!) into folded nori and dunking them in soy sauce. Mike and I love making bowls with the fish, which is generally lightly seared for him and raw for me. Solomon just gobbles up sushi rice and chopped-up pieces of cooked fish and edamame, obviously getting the sticky rice ALL over the kitchen. Regardless of the mess, it's truly the best meal, because everyone is happy and it's so easy to prep! You'll also love the Pineapple Chicken, because it's made on a sheet pan and way more delicious (and healthier) than your local takeout version. Did I mention I've created the best mac and cheese recipe that cooks all in ONE pot? You don't even need to dirty up a colander. Grab your groceries and get going on this one.

THIS WEEK'S MENU

- **Poke Bowls** *with* **Ponzu Sauce**

- **Pineapple Chicken** *with* **Broccoli, Edamame,** *and* **Rice**

- **Loaded Vegetarian Chili Bowls**

- **One-Pot Mac** *and* **Cheese** *with* **Broccoli**

PREP

1 Sushi Rice

2 Vegetarian Chili

3 Pineapple Chicken

4 Roasted Broccoli

5 Edamame

6 Poke Marinade

7 Ponzu Sauce

NOTES & SWAPS

PREP SMART

- Buy frozen broccoli or precut broccoli florets to save time.
- Buy carrots and purple cabbage preshredded for easy poke bowl topping.
- Buy store-bought ponzu to eliminate one recipe from your prep.

PREP IT MORE KID-FRIENDLY

- For picky kids, you can serve the chili in crunchy tacos, cook eggs in it to create a delicious shakshuka (like on page 63), make nachos by baking it with tortilla chips, or load it on a hot dog to make chili dogs.

PREP IT GLUTEN-FREE/LIGHTEN IT UP

- Make cauliflower rice or zucchini noodles in place of sushi rice.
- Skip the mac and cheese and instead whip up a cheesy broccoli frittata (see page 265).

PREP IT VEGETARIAN

- Replace chicken with extra vegetables of choice (snap peas, peppers, mushrooms, etc.) or a soy chicken alternative.
- You can use part of the poke marinade for tofu instead of fish. Marinate overnight, dry off well, and bake.

COOKING TOOLS AND EQUIPMENT NEEDED

- Chef's knife
- Cutting board
- Fine-mesh sieve
- Microplane
- Medium (3-quart) saucepan
- Large (6- to 8-quart) stockpot
- Medium bowl
- 1 extra-large baking sheet and 1 standard baking sheet or 3 standard baking sheets
- 9 x 13-inch baking dish
- Tongs
- 2 (16-ounce) storage jars with tight-fitting lids

GROCERY LIST

PRODUCE

- 2 onions ② ③
- 7 garlic cloves ② ③
- 1 large red bell pepper ②
- 10 baby carrots ②
- 1 pound sugar snap peas ③
- 2 limes ⑦
- 1 jalapeño (optional) ⑦ + 4 for R
- 1 English cucumber R
- 5 radishes R
- 2 cups shredded carrots R
- 6 scallions R
- 2 cups small-diced pineapple or mango R
- 2 cups shredded purple cabbage R
- 2 avocados R
- 32 ounces (about 12 cups) broccoli florets ④

PANTRY

- Light olive oil
- Kosher salt
- Pepper
- 1 tablespoon mild chili powder ②
- 3½ teaspoons garlic powder ② ③ ⑤
- 1 tablespoon ground cumin ②
- 3 tablespoons canned chipotle pepper in adobo sauce (optional) ②
- 1 teaspoon onion powder ③
- 1 teaspoon toasted sesame oil ⑥
- ⅓ cup plus 3 tablespoons rice vinegar ① ⑥
- 6 tablespoons pure maple syrup ① ③
- 1½ tablespoons cornstarch ③
- 2 cups sushi rice ①
- 1 (28-ounce) can fire-roasted diced tomatoes ②
- 1 (28-ounce) can crushed tomatoes ②
- 1 (15.5-ounce) can chickpeas ②
- 1 (20.5-ounce) can pinto beans ②
- 1 (15-ounce) can kidney beans ②
- 1 cup natural canned pineapple chunks in 100% juice + ¾ cup juice from the can ③
- 1 cup low-sodium soy sauce ③ ⑥ ⑦
  + more for R
- ½ teaspoon black sesame seeds ⑥
  + more for R
- Seaweed snacks or toasted nori R
- Optional: Hot sauce (I like Frank's RedHot or Cholula) R
- ½ cup sliced black olives R
- 16 ounces elbow pasta R
- 1 (7.5-ounce) bag corn chips R
- 2 tablespoons all-purpose flour R

DAIRY/FROZEN

- 24 ounces frozen shelled edamame ⑤
- 1 cup sour cream R
- 2 cups shredded cheddar cheese R
- 2 tablespoons unsalted butter R
- 3 cups whole milk R
- 1½ cups shredded mozzarella cheese R

PROTEIN

- 2 pounds boneless, skinless chicken breasts or thighs ③
- 2 pounds tuna steaks (highest-quality sushi-grade, if eating raw) R

*The "R" symbolizes ingredients you'll be using to Rally throughout the week—these won't be needed in the Sunday prep!

PREP

Time to prep! Set aside about an hour on your Prep day to make these recipes, then store them to use for Rally meals during the week.

1 Sushi Rice

MAKES ABOUT 4 CUPS

2 cups uncooked sushi rice

2½ cups water

¾ teaspoon kosher salt

⅓ cup rice vinegar

2 tablespoons pure maple syrup

1 Place the rice in a fine-mesh sieve and rinse it under cold running water for 1 to 2 minutes, until the water runs completely clear. Swirl the rice around with your fingers to thoroughly wash off the excess starch. This is an important step!

2 Combine the rice, water, and salt in a medium saucepan and bring to a boil over high heat. Reduce the heat to maintain a simmer, cover with a tight-fitting lid, and cook for 15 minutes. Remove from the heat and leave covered to steam for 10 minutes longer.

3 Mix in the vinegar and maple syrup. Let cool, then store, covered, in the fridge.

HOT TIP

• Make sure the saucepan used to cook your grains has a tight-fitting lid without a hole at the top to release steam. You want all that steam to stay inside. You can always plug up the hole with some aluminum foil if needed!

2 Vegetarian Chili

SERVES 8

In a large stockpot, heat the oil over high heat. Add the onion and garlic and cook for 5 to 6 minutes, until translucent. Add the pepper and carrots and cook, stirring, for 8 minutes more, until soft. Add the diced tomatoes, crushed tomatoes, chickpeas, pinto beans, kidney beans, chili powder, cumin, garlic powder, salt, and chipotle and stir to combine. Bring to a boil, then reduce the heat to maintain a simmer. Cover and cook for 35 to 40 minutes. Let cool, then store, covered, in the fridge.

2 tablespoons light olive oil

1 onion, finely diced

3 garlic cloves, minced

1 large red bell pepper, finely diced

10 baby carrots, halved lengthwise and finely diced

1 (28-ounce) can fire-roasted diced tomatoes

1 (28-ounce) can crushed tomatoes

1 (15.5-ounce) can chickpeas, drained and rinsed

1 (20.5-ounce) can pinto beans, drained and rinsed

1 (15-ounce) can kidney beans, drained and rinsed

1 tablespoon mild chili powder

1 tablespoon ground cumin

2 teaspoons garlic powder

2 teaspoons kosher salt

3 tablespoons finely chopped canned chipotle pepper in adobo sauce (optional, but highly recommended to add heat and smokiness)

HOT TIPS

- You can make this chili with ground chicken, ground turkey, ground beef, or Beyond Beef; brown the meat as the first step, before adding the onion and garlic.

- If you don't want to make the whole pot of chili spicy, cook it without the chipotle, then add chipotle to individual bowls when serving. For less spice, add only the chipotle sauce and not the actual chopped pepper.

Alternatively, you can cook the chili with a whole California dried pepper in the pot for some smoky yet mild flavor. Discard the pepper (or remove the pepper to a blender and pulse until smooth, then add back into the chili) and serve.

- If you have leftovers, be sure to freeze for a later time—it freezes beautifully. I also love making shakshuka out of the leftovers.

3 Pineapple Chicken

SERVES 4

2 pounds boneless, skinless chicken breasts or thighs, cut into thin strips or chunks

1½ tablespoons cornstarch

1½ teaspoons kosher salt

1 onion, thinly sliced

1 pound sugar snap peas, cut on an angle into thirds

4 garlic cloves, minced

1 teaspoon onion powder

1 teaspoon garlic powder

¼ cup pure maple syrup

¼ cup low-sodium soy sauce

2 tablespoons light olive oil

1 cup natural canned pineapple chunks (in 100% juice), plus ¾ cup juice from the can

1 Preheat the oven to 425°F and set aside a standard baking sheet.

2 In a medium bowl or on a cutting board, toss the chicken with the cornstarch and salt to fully coat, then place the chicken directly on the baking sheet. Add the onion and sugar snap peas on the baking sheet as well. Sprinkle all the ingredients evenly with the minced garlic, onion powder, garlic powder, maple syrup, soy sauce, olive oil, pineapple chunks, and pineapple juice. Massage everything together until evenly distributed. Roast on the top rack for about 20 minutes, rotating the pan halfway through to ensure it cooks evenly. Remove from the oven and give it a nice mix. The sauce will thicken as you mix it together. Let cool, then store, covered, in the fridge.

HOT TIPS

- If you prefer to cook this fresh the day it's served, simply prep everything and store it in the fridge. When you're ready to cook, pour it out onto the baking sheet to cook fresh.

- I love cutting the chicken into thin strips here, but cubes work well too. Cutting your chicken when it's semi-frozen makes it much easier.

- Coating the chicken separately in the cornstarch and salt keeps the chicken super moist and gives the dish that classic Chinese takeout texture and flavor. Don't skip that step! Use arrowroot powder if you don't like cornstarch.

- Replace the chicken with a soy chicken alternative or extra veggies of choice to make it vegetarian!

4

Roasted Broccoli

SERVES 8

Preheat the oven to 425°F. Line one extra-large baking sheet or two standard baking sheets with parchment paper. Spread the broccoli over the prepared pan(s), drizzle with the oil, and season with salt. Roast for 35 minutes. Let cool, then store, covered, in the fridge.

12 cups (2 pounds) broccoli florets

2 to 3 tablespoons light olive oil

Kosher salt

HOT TIP

- If you love steamed broccoli, use that method of preparation here. It's easy and holds up beautifully in the fridge. Simply place a steaming basket in a large stockpot with a splash of water and cook over medium-high heat to steam for 6 to 8 minutes until bright green in color.

5

Edamame

SERVES 4

Preheat the oven to 425°F. Place the edamame in a 9 x 13-inch baking dish and coat with the oil. Season with the garlic powder, salt, and pepper. Roast, covered, for 10 to 15 minutes. Let cool, then store, covered, in the fridge.

24 ounces shelled frozen edamame

1 tablespoon light olive oil

½ teaspoon garlic powder

Kosher salt and pepper

HOT TIP

- These cook quickly and can easily be steamed, air fried, or sautéed fresh to serve if you prefer to skip it during your prep.

6 Poke Marinade

MAKES ABOUT ½ CUP

¼ cup low-sodium soy sauce

3 tablespoons rice vinegar

1 teaspoon toasted sesame oil

½ teaspoon black sesame seeds

Squeeze of hot sauce and/
or mayonnaise (optional, if
you prefer it creamier and
want an even more addicting
marinade)

Combine the soy sauce, vinegar, sesame oil, sesame seeds,
and hot sauce in a medium storage jar. Cover and shake to
mix. Store in the fridge.

7 Ponzu Sauce

MAKES ABOUT ½ CUP

½ cup low-sodium soy sauce

Zest and juice of 2 limes

Sliced fresh jalapeño (optional)

Combine the soy sauce, lime zest and juice, and jalapeño in
a medium storage jar, cover, and shake to mix. Store in the
fridge.

RALLY

Get ready to Rally! Time to take all those
Prep staples and use them to
create delicious meals for the week.

Poke Bowls *with* Ponzu Sauce

SERVES 4

1 Preheat oven to 300°F. Add a splash of water to half of the rice in an oven-safe storage container (reserve the rest for later in the week) and heat, covered, for 15 minutes, until warmed through.

2 Meanwhile, prepare the fish. If eating the tuna raw, cut it into ½-inch cubes, place in a medium bowl, and coat in the marinade. Let marinate for 15 minutes before serving.

3 If you're searing the fish, place whole tuna steaks in the marinade and marinate for 15 to 20 minutes. Remove the fish from the marinade and dry off well on a paper towel and discard marinade. Season both sides with salt and pepper. When ready to cook, heat 2 tablespoons oil in a large nonstick skillet over high heat (let it get very hot before adding the fish) and sear both sides until golden brown, 3 to 4 minutes per side or until golden on the outside but still slightly pink in the center. Let rest before slicing.

4 Display bowls with vegetable add-ins on the table and let everyone top their warmed rice with fish, toppings, and ponzu sauce (reserving some for the Pineapple Chicken). Serve with nori on the side or crumbled in the bowl.

RALLY INGREDIENTS

½ recipe Sushi Rice (page 94)

Poke Marinade (page 98)

Ponzu Sauce (page 98)

½ recipe Edamame (page 97)

ADDITIONAL INGREDIENTS

2 pounds tuna steaks (highest-quality sushi-grade, if eating raw)

Kosher salt and pepper

Light olive oil (if frying)

1 English cucumber, thinly sliced

5 radishes, thinly sliced

2 cups shredded carrots

3 scallions, thinly sliced

2 cups finely diced pineapple or mango

2 cups shredded purple cabbage

Black sesame seeds, for topping

Toasted nori or seaweed snacks, for serving

RALLY REMEDIES

• Let the kids make nori tacos by loading rice into individual seaweed snacks with toppings and holding them like tacos. You can also make sushi if you want to get fancy!

• To make this vegetarian, marinate tofu steaks overnight and sear the tofu like you would cook the tuna steaks. You can also broil it.

• Serve with cauliflower rice, zucchini noodles, or mixed greens instead of rice to lighten up this meal.

Pineapple Chicken *with* Broccoli, Edamame, *and* Rice

SERVES 4

RALLY INGREDIENTS

Pineapple Chicken (page 96)

½ recipe Sushi Rice (page 94)

Roasted Broccoli (page 97; reserve 3 cups for Thursday)

½ recipe Edamame (page 97)

Leftover Ponzu Sauce (page 98; optional)

Preheat oven to 300°F. Heat the pineapple chicken and rice, covered, in oven-safe storage containers for 20 to 30 minutes, until warmed through. Heat the broccoli and edamame, uncovered, in oven-safe storage containers in the same oven for 15 minutes, until warm. Serve all together topped with ponzu sauce, if desired.

RALLY REMEDY

- Try making a fried rice following the general method from Salami and Egg Fried Rice (see page 268), but using the broccoli and edamame. This is a different way to serve this meal if someone doesn't want the pineapple chicken. It's also a great vegetarian option.

- To make this dinner extra fun, serve it with chopsticks and Chinese takeout boxes. Your kids will love it and cleanup will be a breeze!

Loaded Vegetarian Chili Bowls

SERVES 4 TO 6

Put the chili in a stockpot if it isn't already, cover, and heat over low heat, stirring occasionally, until warmed through. Meanwhile, assemble all the toppings in individual bowls on the table. Serve the chili hot and add toppings as desired!

RALLY INGREDIENTS

Vegetarian Chili (page 95)

ADDITIONAL INGREDIENTS

1 (7.5-ounce) bag corn chips

1 cup sour cream

2 cups shredded cheddar cheese

2 avocados, cubed

3 scallions, thinly sliced

½ cup sliced black olives

Hot sauce

1 jalapeño, thinly sliced

Canned chipotle pepper in adobo sauce, peppers finely chopped, or just the sauce, for serving (optional)

RALLY REMEDIES

- I love serving this like nachos! Spread tortilla chips out on a baking sheet. Top with chili, cheese, and other toppings of choice, and bake at 400°F for 10 to 15 minutes, until hot and bubbling. Kids love these!

- When in doubt, make shakshuka! Place some chili in a shallow skillet or Dutch oven and bring to a simmer, then crack eggs into the chili and cook until the eggs have reached the desired doneness, 5 to 8 minutes. Alternatively, serve the chili over hot dogs or vegan alternative!

One-Pot Mac *and* Cheese *with* Broccoli

SERVES 4 TO 6

RALLY INGREDIENTS

3 cups Roasted Broccoli, or all
   remaining (page 97)

ADDITIONAL INGREDIENTS

2 tablespoons unsalted butter

2 tablespoons all-purpose flour

3 cups whole milk

2 cups water

1½ teaspoons kosher salt

16 ounces elbow pasta

1½ cups shredded mozzarella
   cheese

Hot sauce (I like Frank's RedHot
   or Cholula; optional)

1 In a medium stockpot, melt the butter over high heat. Add the flour and whisk until it looks like a smooth paste. Immediately add the milk, water, and salt and whisk until smooth. Add the pasta and mix to submerge everything in the liquid. Bring just to a boil, then immediately reduce the heat to a simmer (there should be little bubbles present as it's simmering). Cook, uncovered, stirring every few minutes, until most of the liquid has been absorbed and the pasta is al dente, about 8 minutes. Keep an eye on it to ensure it doesn't boil over!

2 Add the cheese and stir until fully melted and creamy, then remove from heat. Chop the broccoli and stir it right into the mac and cheese, or warm it up to serve as a side dish. Serve immediately, topped with hot sauce for the spice lovers.

RALLY REMEDIES

- Make a broccoli frittata (see page 265) to make this a lighter meal.

- This recipe will work with most pasta varieties that require an 8 to 9 minute cook time. You can also make a simple béchamel (white cream) sauce and add any cooked pasta in separately. Follow all the sauce ingredients but omit the 2 cups of water. Simmer until thickened and smooth.

- If you've got some nutmeg on hand and want to take this to the next level, add ¼ teaspoon to the pot! I even like it with a squeeze of mustard to really amp up the flavors.

CHAPTER 5

No Way It's Veg

MAKES: 4 DINNERS FOR 4 PEOPLE

I get many requests for fully vegetarian menus on prepandrally.com, and even though my menus can always be modified to be vegetarian, I wanted to include one menu that was designed to be plant-based. This menu is playful and bursting with flavor. If you want to swap in some meat for the burgers to please your crew, go ahead and do what works for you, but you definitely won't be missing the meat here!

- **Shepherd's Pie** *with* **Polenta Crust** *and* **Green Beans**

- **Vegetarian Sheet Pan Fajitas** *with* **Chipotle-Lime Crema** *and* **Green Beans**

- **Veggie Burgers** *with* **Chipotle-Lime Crema** *and* **Polenta Fries**

- **Smashed Tomato Fusilli**

PREP

1. **Sheet Pan Fajitas**
2. **Roasted Green Beans**
3. **Shepherd's Pie**
4. **Veggie Burger Mixture**
5. **Polenta**
6. **Smashed Tomato Sauce**
7. **Chipotle-Lime Crema**

NOTES & SWAPS

PREP SMART

- You can use thawed and drained frozen vegetables of choice for the shepherd's pie to save lots of time on chopping and dicing.
- Use an all-purpose taco spice blend for the fajitas and chipotle-lime crema to save time on adding multiple spices!
- To score some breakfast while you're at it, make breakfast burritos with this week's leftovers: Take some of the fajita mixture, combine it with some of the shepherd's pie filling (without the polenta topping), and warm it in a pan. Scramble an egg and roll it all up into a burrito. Best breakfast ever!
- Reserve the whole pasta recipe for later in the week to save even more prep time. You can even just use store-bought tomato sauce and make a baked ziti instead, if you prefer.

PREP IT MORE KID-FRIENDLY

- Feel free to make beef burgers instead of veggie, or use Beyond Burger meat to keep it vegetarian.
- Instead of the artichokes, feel free to use chicken (or a soy chicken replacement) in the fajitas.

PREP IT GLUTEN-FREE/LIGHTEN IT UP

- Don't like polenta? No problem. Bake the shepherd's pie topped with a sheet of gluten-free pie dough or even additional mashed potatoes or sweet potatoes, more like a traditional shepherd's pie. Instead of the polenta fries, you can make regular potato fries or even turnip fries (see page 175).
- Use chickpea, lentil, or brown rice pasta in place of the fusilli to make it gluten-free; spaghetti squash is delicious here as well.

COOKING TOOLS AND EQUIPMENT NEEDED

- Chef's knife
- Cutting board
- 9 x 13-inch baking dish
- 4 standard baking sheets
- Microplane
- Large (12-inch) sauté pan
- 4-quart saucepan
- Medium (6-inch) skillet
- 16-ounce storage jar with lid
- Vegetable peeler
- Large storage bowl with lid
- Fork, potato masher, or salad chopper

GROCERY LIST

PRODUCE

- 2 large onions **1** **3**
- 1 large red bell pepper **1**
- 1 large yellow pepper **1**
- 4 scallions **4**
- 2 limes **1** **7** + 2 limes R
- 1½ pounds green beans **2**
- 1 medium russet potato **3**
- 1 medium sweet potato **3**
- 1 cup baby carrots **3**
- 2 celery stalks **3**
- 14 ounces sliced white button mushrooms **3** **4**
- 5 ounces sliced shiitake mushrooms **4**
- 6 garlic cloves **6**
- 20 ounces cherry tomatoes **6**
- 6 ounces baby spinach **6**
- 1 jalapeño (optional) R
- 1½ cups shredded romaine lettuce R
- 1 lemon R
- 1 large ripe tomato R
- 1 head butter lettuce R
- 1 bunch parsley R
- 2 avocados R

PANTRY

- Light olive oil
- Kosher salt
- Pepper
- 4 teaspoons garlic powder **1** **3** + 1 teaspoon R
- 1 teaspoon ground cumin **1**
- 3 teaspoons mild chili powder **1** **7**
- 3 teaspoons oregano **1** **3** **6**
- 3 teaspoons sweet paprika **1** **3**
- 1 tablespoon balsamic vinegar **3**

- 2 tablespoons low-sodium soy sauce **3** + 2 tablespoons R
- 3 tablespoons tomato paste **3**
- Hot sauce or canned chipotle peppers in adobo sauce (optional) **7**
- 2 (14-ounce) cans artichoke bottoms or quartered artichoke hearts **1**
- 2½ cups vegetable stock **3**
- 1 (15-ounce) can cannellini beans **3**
- 1 (15.5-ounce) can black beans, drained and rinsed **4**
- 2 tablespoons capers **6**
- 2 cups coarse cornmeal **5**
- ¼ cup mayonnaise **7**
- 2 tablespoons tahini R
- 16 ounces fusilli pasta R
- Red pepper flakes (optional) R
- ¾ cup rolled oats R
- 6 to 8 flour or corn tortillas R
- 4 to 6 burger buns R

DAIRY

- ½ cup grated Parmesan cheese **5** + 1¼ cups R
- ½ cup sour cream **7**
- 1 large egg R
- ⅓ cup shredded cheddar cheese R

*The "R" symbolizes ingredients you'll be using to Rally throughout the week—these won't be needed in the Sunday prep!

PREP

Time to prep! Set aside about an hour on your Prep day to make these recipes, then store them to use for Rally meals during the week.

1 Sheet Pan Fajitas

SERVES 4

2 (14-ounce) cans artichoke bottoms or quartered artichoke hearts

1 onion, halved and thinly sliced

1 large red bell pepper, cut into ½-inch-wide strips

1 large yellow pepper, cut into ½-inch-wide strips

3 tablespoons light olive oil

2 teaspoons garlic powder

2 teaspoons mild chili powder

2 teaspoons sweet paprika

1½ teaspoons kosher salt

1 teaspoon ground cumin

1 teaspoon dried oregano

½ teaspoon pepper

Zest and juice of 1 lime

Preheat the oven to 425°F. Line a standard baking sheet with parchment paper. If you're using artichoke bottoms, cut each into ½-inch strips. Combine the artichokes, onion, and bell peppers on the baking sheet, drizzle with the oil, and toss to coat. Season with the garlic powder, chili powder, paprika, salt, cumin, oregano, pepper, and lime zest and juice and toss again. Roast for 35 minutes on the top rack until golden. Let cool, then store, covered, in the fridge.

HOT TIP

- I love using artichoke bottoms when I'm able to find them at the grocery store, since they look like chicken. You can bump up the protein by using seitan instead of artichokes or use actual chicken cut into strips for a nonvegetarian meal.

2 Roasted Green Beans

SERVES 6

24 ounces green beans

2 to 3 tablespoons light olive oil

Kosher salt and pepper

Preheat the oven to 425°F. Line a standard baking sheet with parchment paper. Spread the green beans over the baking sheet, toss to coat with the oil, and season with salt and pepper. Roast on the top rack for 30 to 35 minutes, or until golden. Let cool, then store, covered, in the fridge.

3 Shepherd's Pie

SERVES 6 TO 8

1 Grease a 9 x 13-inch baking dish with oil.

2 In a large sauté pan, heat the oil over high heat. Add the onion and cook for 5 minutes, until translucent. Add the russet potato, sweet potato, carrots, celery, mushrooms, tomato paste, soy sauce, and vinegar to the pan. Add the garlic powder, salt, oregano, paprika, pepper, and stock. It will seem like a lot of stock, but the potatoes will absorb it all. Bring to a simmer and cook for about 25 minutes, until the potatoes are just softened. Mix in the cannellini beans and then pour the mixture into the prepared baking dish (or keep it in the skillet if it's an oven-safe pan and you want to store and serve the shepherd's pie in it later in the week). Set aside while you make the polenta (see page 117) to use as a topping for the shepherd's pie.

2 to 3 tablespoons light olive oil, plus more for greasing

1 large onion, finely diced

1 medium russet potato, peeled and finely diced (1½ cups)

1 medium sweet potato, peeled and finely diced (1½ cups)

1 cup finely diced baby carrots

2 celery stalks, finely diced (about ½ cup chopped)

8 ounces sliced white button mushrooms, chopped

3 tablespoons tomato paste

2 tablespoons low-sodium soy sauce

1 tablespoon balsamic vinegar

2 teaspoons garlic powder

2 teaspoons kosher salt

1 teaspoon dried oregano

1 teaspoon sweet paprika

¼ teaspoon pepper

2½ cups vegetable stock

1 (15-ounce) can cannellini beans, drained and rinsed

HOT TIPS

• While the potato mixture is cooking, start prepping the veggie burger mixture. Then make the polenta topping for the shepherd's pie.

• The shepherd's pie makes a nice amount that will definitely yield some leftovers. It makes a great breakfast or lunch, and also freezes nicely. Feel free to cut the recipe in half, though, if you'd rather not have leftovers.

• If you're making this as a stand-alone recipe, head to page 121 for cooking directions.

Veggie Burger Mixture

5 ounces sliced shiitake mushrooms, finely diced

6 ounces sliced white button mushrooms, finely diced

1 (15.5-ounce) can black beans, drained and rinsed

4 scallions, finely chopped

2 tablespoons light olive oil

½ teaspoon kosher salt

Preheat the oven to 425°F. Line a standard baking sheet with parchment paper. Arrange the shiitake mushrooms, button mushrooms, black beans, and scallions on the pan. Coat with the oil and salt and roast for 15 minutes. Let cool slightly, then transfer everything to a large storage bowl. Mash the mixture with a fork, potato masher, or salad chopper to break up the beans. Store, covered, in the fridge.

HOT TIP

- If you're making this as a stand-alone recipe, head to page 125 for cooking directions.

Polenta

**MAKES TOPPING FOR 1 SHEPHERD'S PIE
AND 4 SERVINGS FRIES**

1 Make the polenta topping: In a large saucepan, bring the water and salt to a boil. Add the cornmeal and reduce the heat to maintain a simmer, then cook, stirring to incorporate and to avoid lumps, for about 5 minutes. Add the Parmesan and stir until melted, then remove from the heat.

2 Pour 2 cups of the polenta over the shepherd's pie (page 115) and spread it to mostly cover the top. You can also just pour random blobs of the polenta over the top to leave it rustic. Let the polenta cool, then cover the shepherd's pie with aluminum foil or plastic wrap and store in the fridge.

3 Make the fries: Line a standard baking sheet with parchment paper and spray or coat the parchment with oil. Pour the remaining polenta onto the baking sheet and spread it into an even layer about ½ inch thick. Let cool, then cover with plastic wrap and store in the fridge.

6 cups water

2 teaspoons kosher salt

2 cups coarse cornmeal

½ cup grated Parmesan cheese

Cooking oil spray or light olive oil, for greasing

HOT TIPS

- If you're making the polenta fries as a stand-alone recipe, only cook 1½ cups coarse cornmeal with 4½ cups water, then head to page 125 for cooking directions.

- You can swap out the Parmesan for shredded mozzarella, if you prefer, or omit the cheese completely if needed.

- If you want to make a simple pot of polenta, follow the directions in the first step here and serve bowls of creamy polenta topped with sautéed or roasted vegetables and a 7-minute egg (see page 266) for a simple and comforting dinner. It's also delicious topped with barbacoa (see page 194).

- The polenta will thicken as it cools, but you can always make it creamy again by simmering it with more water.

6 Smashed Tomato Sauce

SERVES 4

3 tablespoons light olive oil

6 garlic cloves, minced

20 ounces cherry tomatoes

1 teaspoon dried oregano

Kosher salt and pepper

2 tablespoons capers, drained and coarsely chopped

6 ounces baby spinach

In a medium skillet, heat the oil over medium heat. Add the garlic and cook, stirring, for 1 to 2 minutes, being careful not to burn it. Add the tomatoes, season with the oregano, salt, and pepper, and cook for 7 to 8 minutes, until the tomatoes have burst. Add the capers and spinach and cook, stirring, for another minute or two, until the spinach has wilted. Let cool, then store, covered, in the fridge.

HOT TIP

- Blend the smashed tomato sauce to make it look like a smooth sauce for pickier eaters. You can also omit the spinach if needed.

- If you're making this as a stand-alone recipe, head to page 126 for cooking directions.

7 Chipotle-Lime Crema

MAKES ABOUT 1 CUP

½ cup sour cream

¼ cup mayonnaise

Zest and juice of 1 lime (2 tablespoons juice)

1 teaspoon mild chili powder, or 1 tablespoon of the sauce from canned chipotle peppers in adobo, if you like heat

Squirt of hot sauce (optional)

Kosher salt

Combine the sour cream, mayo, lime zest and juice, chili powder, and hot sauce (if using) in a storage jar. Whisk to combine and season with salt. Cover and store in the fridge.

RALLY

Get ready to Rally! Time to take all those Prep staples and use them to create delicious meals for the week.

Shepherd's Pie *with* Polenta Crust *and* Green Beans

SERVES 6 TO 8

1 Heat the oven to 400°F. Remove the shepherd's pie from the fridge. Bake, covered, for 30 to 35 minutes, until all the liquid has been absorbed and the top is bubbling and golden.

2 Place the green beans on a baking sheet and heat, uncovered, in the same oven for 15 minutes, or until warmed through. Serve the green beans and shepherd's pie family-style.

RALLY INGREDIENTS

Shepherd's Pie (page 115)

½ recipe Roasted Green Beans (page 114)

RALLY REMEDIES

• Freeze leftover shepherd's pie for the most perfect dinner another night. It freezes beautifully.

• Roll the shepherd's pie into a breakfast burrito to serve it differently. Add some scrambled eggs too!

Vegetarian Sheet Pan Fajitas *with* Chipotle-Lime Crema *and* Green Beans

SERVES 4

RALLY INGREDIENTS

Sheet Pan Fajitas (page 114)

½ recipe Roasted Green Beans (page 114)

½ recipe Chipotle-Lime Crema (page 118)

ADDITIONAL INGREDIENTS

6 to 8 flour or corn tortillas

2 limes

Thinly sliced jalapeño (optional)

1½ cups shredded romaine lettuce

2 ripe avocados, mashed

Preheat the oven to 300°F. Heat the fajita mixture, uncovered, in an oven-safe storage container for 25 to 30 minutes, until warmed through. Heat the green beans, uncovered, in an oven-safe container in the same oven for 20 minutes, or until warm. Set up a fajita bar by warming or charring the tortillas and putting out the crema, limes, jalapeño, lettuce, and mashed avocado in individual bowls. Serve with the green beans as a side dish.

RALLY REMEDIES

- Serve the fajita mixture in bowls instead of in tortillas to lighten it up with all the additional fixins.

- Feel free to season up the mashed avocado and turn it into your favorite guacamole.

Veggie Burgers *with* Chipotle-Lime Crema *and* Polenta Fries

SERVES 4

1 Preheat the oven to 450°F.

2 Remove the polenta from the fridge and cut it into ¼-inch-thick fries. Arrange them on a baking sheet so none are touching. Spray with cooking oil and roast until crisp, 25 to 30 minutes.

3 Meanwhile, make the burgers: Remove the veggie burger mixture from the fridge. Add the oats, cheese, tahini, soy sauce, egg, garlic powder, and salt. Mix together, mashing the beans with a fork (see Rally Remedies for details) so the burgers will hold together. Form the mixture into 5 or 6 patties.

4 In a medium skillet, heat the oil over medium-high heat. Fry the burgers until golden and crisp on both sides, 3 to 4 minutes. Flip back to the original side and cook for 3 minutes or so more to make sure the center is fully cooked through.

5 If desired, mix together the Parmesan and parsley and use this to top the fries right when they come out of the oven.

6 Serve the burgers in buns, topped with lettuce, tomato, and crema, with the fries alongside.

RALLY REMEDIES

- I like using a salad chopper to chop the ingredients for veggie burgers. For pickier kids, pulse some of the mixture in a food processor so it looks more like beef burger.

- To bake, place patties on a greased standard baking sheet. Spray the tops with more oil and bake at 450°F for 15 to 20 minutes.

- Serve the burgers with ketchup for picky kids. Serve in iceberg lettuce cups for a super-refreshing and light meal.

RALLY INGREDIENTS

Polenta on the baking sheet to make fries (page 117)

Veggie Burger Mixture (page 116)

½ recipe Chipotle-Lime Crema (page 118)

ADDITIONAL INGREDIENTS

Cooking oil spray

FOR THE BURGERS

¾ cup rolled oats

⅓ cup shredded cheddar cheese

2 tablespoons tahini

2 tablespoons low-sodium soy sauce

1 large egg

1 teaspoon garlic powder

¾ teaspoon kosher salt

2 tablespoons light olive oil

FOR SERVING

¼ cup Parmesan cheese (optional)

¼ cup chopped fresh parsley (optional)

4 to 6 burger buns

1 head butter lettuce

1 ripe large tomato, sliced

Smashed Tomato Fusilli

SERVES 4 TO 6

RALLY INGREDIENTS

Smashed Tomato Sauce
  (page 118)

ADDITIONAL INGREDIENTS

Kosher salt

16 ounces fusilli pasta

1 cup grated Parmesan cheese

Juice of 1 lemon

Pepper

Red chile flakes (optional)

1 Fill a large saucepan three-quarters full with water and season with a big pinch of salt. Bring to a boil over high heat. Add the pasta and cook for 8 minutes or so, until al dente. Drain in a colander without rinsing.

2 Pour the tomato sauce into the same saucepan you used to cook the pasta and heat it over medium heat for 3 to 4 minutes to warm through. Add the pasta to the sauce and mix to coat. Finish with Parmesan and lemon juice to taste and season with salt and black pepper as needed.

3 Top with red chile flakes, if you like, and serve.

RALLY REMEDIES

• Use gluten-free pasta as needed here.

• Make a quick side salad to go along with the pasta using any of this week's leftover produce.

• To avoid pasta altogether, sauté up some zucchini noodles to serve with the smashed tomato sauce.

CHAPTER 6

Winter Cozies

MAKES: 4 DINNERS FOR 4 PEOPLE

This meal plan is all about comfort food! I love prepping this menu in the winter when I want cozy and comforting meals on those cool days (not like we get many of those out here in LA!). We're repurposing the couscous in two different meals to save some time—plus, I'm sharing a fun way to make fish sticks the ~~lazy~~ Prep + Rally way!

- **Hasselback Salmon, Chimichurri,** *and* **Parmesan Roasted Broccoli** *with* **Salad** *and* **Tangy Vinaigrette**

- **Chicken Curry** *over* **Couscous**

- **Saucy Meat Stuffed Shells** *with* **Roasted Squash**

- **Cheesy Couscous Risotto** *with* **Peas** *and* **Broccoli**

PREP

1. **Chicken Curry**
2. **Roasted Squash**
3. **Roasted Broccoli**
4. **Hasselback Salmon**
5. **Saucy Meat**
6. **Pasta Shells**
7. **Couscous**
8. **Chimichurri**
9. **Tangy Vinaigrette**

NOTES & SWAPS

PREP SMART

- Squash is a super seasonal ingredient. If you can't find acorn squash, sub in another one you like, such as delicata, butternut, kabocha, etc. You can even buy precut butternut squash fries and roast them like French fries.

PREP IT MORE KID-FRIENDLY

- Once the risotto is prepared, mix in one egg and place dollops on a greased skillet. Fry like patties until golden on both sides for an even more kid-friendly dish.
- Can't find jumbo shells, or prefer other pasta? Use shapes your kids like, such as pinwheels or bow ties. Serve the dish as a pasta in meat sauce.

PREP IT GLUTEN-FREE/LIGHTEN IT UP

- Omit the pasta shells and serve the roasted acorn squash along with the saucy meat. Alternatively, you can buy a gluten-free spaghetti or pasta!
- Replace the couscous with cooked white beans, gluten-free pasta, spaghetti squash, or cauliflower rice.

PREP IT VEGETARIAN

- Make the curry vegetarian by swapping in tofu for the chicken. I love loading the curry with cauliflower, potatoes, and chickpeas, too, for a super-flavorful and comforting vegetarian meal.
- Use cauliflower rice in place of the meat when prepping the saucy meat. You can use that as a filling for the shells and sprinkle some shredded cheese over the top when heating it up.
- Use the bread crumb topping for the salmon to coat zucchini sticks or eggplant slices instead of the fish. Follow the eggplant version of chicken katsu (page 219).

COOKING TOOLS AND EQUIPMENT NEEDED

- Chef's knife
- Cutting board
- Medium stockpot or large sauté pan
- 1 extra-large baking sheet and 2 standard baking sheets, or 5 standard baking sheets
- 8-quart stockpot
- 6-quart stockpot
- Microplane
- 32-ounce wide-mouthed jar with lid
- 16-ounce wide-mouthed jar with lid
- Immersion blender or high-powered blender
- Colander
- Fine-mesh sieve
- 1 medium mixing bowl
- 1 large sauté pan

1 Chicken Curry

SERVES 4

2 tablespoons light olive oil

1 onion, diced

1 red bell pepper, thinly sliced

3 garlic cloves, minced

2 pounds boneless, skinless chicken breasts or thighs, cut into 1-inch cubes

1 tablespoon mild curry powder

2 teaspoons kosher salt

1½ teaspoons garlic powder

1 teaspoon sweet paprika

½ teaspoon dried oregano

3 tablespoons tomato paste

1 (13.5-ounce) can full-fat coconut milk

Juice of 2 limes (about ¼ cup)

1½ cups diced frozen carrots and peas (12 ounces)

1 In a medium stockpot or large sauté pan, heat the oil over medium-high heat. Add the onion, bell pepper, and garlic and sauté for 5 to 6 minutes, until softened. Add the chicken, curry powder, salt, garlic powder, paprika, and oregano and cook until the chicken is mostly cooked through, 8 to 10 minutes.

2 Add the tomato paste, coconut milk, and lime juice and bring to a boil. Reduce the heat to maintain a simmer and cook, uncovered, for 5 minutes or so more, until the sauce has thickened. Mix in the carrots and peas and let cool, then store, covered, in the fridge.

HOT TIP

• To make this vegetarian, replace the chicken with tofu: Cube up extra-firm tofu, dry off well, and coat it in a few tablespoons of cornstarch and some salt. Fry in oil in a nonstick skillet until crisp and golden on all sides. Add the remaining ingredients and cook according to the Chicken Curry recipe directions. Alternatively, you can use seitan and/or throw in cauliflower florets, finely diced potato, and chickpeas.

2 Roasted Squash

SERVES 4 OR 5

Preheat the oven to 425°F. Line a standard baking sheet with parchment paper. Arrange the squash slices on the baking sheet, drizzle with the oil, and season with salt and pepper. Roast for about 35 minutes, until softened and cooked through. Remove from the oven and place in a storage container. Let cool, then store, covered, in the fridge.

3 acorn squash, halved, seeded, and cut horizontally into 1-inch-thick slices

3 to 4 tablespoons light olive oil

Kosher salt and pepper

HOT TIP

• Winter squashes like acorn squash are tough to cut through, and cutting up the acorn squash takes some time. Cut the squash in half, remove the seeds, and cook it that way, increasing the cook time slightly. The slices simply make it more fun to eat and create a cute flower shape kids love and the skin is completely edible.

3 Roasted Broccoli

SERVES 8

Preheat the oven to 425°F. Line an extra-large baking sheet or two standard baking sheets with parchment paper. Spread the broccoli over the prepared pan(s), coat with the oil, and season with salt. Roast for 15 minutes (you will be adding the Parmesan to it later in the week, so don't overcook now). Let cool, then store, covered, in the fridge.

10 cups (about 32 ounces) broccoli florets

2 to 3 tablespoons light olive oil

Kosher salt

HOT TIP

• Not as much of a broccoli fan as my family is? Feel free to swap it out for your favorite vegetable: Broccolini, cauliflower, green beans, etc.

Hasselback Salmon

SERVES 5 TO 6

1 (2-pound) skin-on side of salmon, bones removed

1½ teaspoons kosher salt

¼ teaspoon pepper

½ cup panko bread crumbs

¾ cup finely grated Parmesan cheese

1 teaspoon garlic powder

Zest of 1 lemon

2 to 3 tablespoons light olive oil, or cooking oil spray

1 Line a standard baking sheet with parchment paper and add the salmon flesh side up. Using a sharp knife, make about 15 horizontal slits in the salmon, being careful to cut just to the skin but not through it. Make one long cut lengthwise down the center of the salmon (still ensuring you cut just to the skin and not through it) so you end up with 30 small "fish sticks." Season the fish with 1 teaspoon of the salt and the pepper.

2 In a medium bowl, mix together the panko, Parmesan, garlic powder, lemon zest, and remaining ½ teaspoon salt. (Save the rest of the lemon to serve with the fish later in the week.)

3 Sprinkle the panko mixture all over the top of the fish and in all the cuts and grooves you made, pressing to adhere to the salmon. Drizzle the top with the oil or spray with cooking oil and cover tightly with plastic wrap or aluminum foil. Store in the fridge overnight to cook fresh just prior to serving.

HOT TIPS

• My kids love this as is, but you can add a nice coating of honey mustard before adding the bread crumbs for a slightly different—yet equally delicious—version of this dish.

• To make this vegetarian, make the eggplant version of chicken katsu (page 219) but cut the eggplant planks into sticks so they are dunkable. You can also add some Parmesan to the panko mixture Do the same with zucchini sticks.

• If you're making this as a stand-alone recipe, head to page 143 for cooking directions.

5 **Saucy Meat**

SERVES 4

2 tablespoons light olive oil

1 onion, finely diced

3 garlic cloves, minced

2 pounds ground beef

1 tablespoon sweet paprika

2 teaspoons garlic powder

2 teaspoons onion powder

1½ teaspoons kosher salt

1 teaspoon dried oregano

½ teaspoon ground turmeric

2 tablespoons tomato paste

1 (15-ounce) can crushed tomatoes

In a large sauté pan, heat the oil over high heat. Add the onion and garlic and cook, stirring, until softened and golden, 1 to 2 minutes. Add the ground beef, paprika, garlic powder, onion powder, salt, oregano, and turmeric. Cook, breaking up the meat with a spatula as it cooks, until fully browned, 5 minutes or so. Add the tomato paste and crushed tomatoes and bring to a simmer, then cook for 5 to 8 minutes more, until everything is cooked through, thickened, and incorporated. Let cool, then store, covered, in the fridge.

HOT TIP

- I love stirring grated zucchini, grated carrots, and finely diced mushrooms into my meat sauce in addition to the meat, or using them to replace the meat altogether. It's a great way to make this sauce vegetarian and increase your family's vegetable intake! You can also use Beyond Beef.

6 Pasta Shells

SERVES 4

Fill a large stockpot halfway with water and season liberally with salt. Bring the water to a boil over high heat. Add the shells and cook according to the package directions until al dente. Drain, rinse, and place in a storage container. Massage the shells with a little oil to keep the noodles from sticking to each other. Cover and store in the fridge.

Kosher salt

12 jumbo pasta shells

Light olive oil, for greasing

HOT TIP

- Save a few steps during your prep and make the pasta and couscous later in the week.

7 Couscous

SERVES 8

Fill a medium stockpot three-quarters of the way with water, season liberally with salt, and bring to a boil over high heat. Add the oil and couscous, then bring back to a boil. Reduce the heat to maintain a simmer and cook, uncovered, for 6 to 7 minutes, until the couscous is al dente. Drain in a fine-mesh sieve and rinse. Place in a storage container and mix in some more oil to keep the grains of couscous from sticking to each other. Let cool, then cover and store in the fridge.

Kosher salt

2 tablespoons light olive oil, plus more for coating

4 cups pearl couscous

8 Chimichurri

MAKES ABOUT 1½ CUPS

2 garlic cloves, peeled

1 cup fresh parsley or cilantro, roughly torn

½ teaspoon dried oregano

½ cup white wine vinegar

⅓ cup extra-virgin olive oil

Kosher salt and pepper

Combine the garlic, parsley, oregano, vinegar, and oil in a wide-mouthed jar and pulse with an immersion blender. I like to leave the texture a little chunky. Season with salt and pepper, cover, and store in the fridge.

HOT TIPS

- I love using leftover chimichurri to serve with grilled steak or BBQ chicken (see page 132). It's also great as a marinade—just omit the vinegar. If you can't use it up this week, scrape it into an ice cube tray and freeze for later use!

- Add a jalapeño for an even more delicious chimichurri.

9 Tangy Vinaigrette

MAKES ABOUT 1 CUP

1 garlic clove, minced

¼ cup white wine vinegar

1 teaspoon Dijon mustard

½ cup extra-virgin olive oil

2 tablespoons honey

½ teaspoon ground turmeric

1 teaspoon dried oregano

Kosher salt and pepper

Combine the garlic, vinegar, mustard, oil, honey, turmeric, oregano, and pinches of salt and pepper in a storage jar. Cover, and shake to mix. Store in the fridge.

RALLY

Get ready to Rally! Time to take all those
Prep staples and use them to
create delicious meals for the week.

Hasselback Salmon, Chimichurri, *and* Parmesan Roasted Broccoli *with* Salad *and* Tangy Vinaigrette

SERVES 4

1 Preheat the oven to 425°F. Remove the salmon from the fridge, uncover, and roast for 30 to 35 minutes, until golden and crisp.

2 Line a standard baking sheet with parchment paper. Place the broccoli on the baking sheet and coat in the Parmesan. Add the broccoli to the oven during the last 10 minutes of the salmon's cook time and roast until the broccoli is warmed through and the Parmesan has melted and become crispy all over.

3 Meanwhile, in a large bowl, combine the lettuce, tomatoes, hearts of palm, and scallions. Toss with the vinaigrette.

4 Serve the salmon on a platter, allowing everyone to pull off nuggets and dunk them in the chimichurri sauce. Squeeze fresh lemon juice over the fish as desired, and serve the salad and broccoli alongside.

RALLY INGREDIENTS

Hasselback Salmon (page 136)

Roasted Broccoli (page 135; reserve 1 to 2 cups for Thursday)

½ recipe Tangy Vinaigrette (page 140)

½ recipe Chimichurri (page 140)

ADDITIONAL INGREDIENTS

½ cup grated Parmesan cheese

1 head romaine or butter lettuce, chopped

3 Roma (plum) tomatoes, chopped

1 (14-ounce) can hearts of palm, sliced into rounds

3 scallions, thinly sliced

1 lemon, cut into wedges, for serving (optional)

RALLY REMEDIES

- Try mixing some chimichurri sauce into mayonnaise for a creamy dip.

- Serve crispy breaded zucchini sticks or eggplant dunked in chimichurri or some marinara sauce if you've prepared a vegetarian option.

Chicken Curry *over* Couscous

SERVES 4

RALLY INGREDIENTS

Chicken Curry (page 134)

Couscous (page 139; reserve
4 cups for Thursday)

ADDITIONAL INGREDIENTS

2 to 3 tablespoons chopped
fresh parsley or cilantro

Unsweetened coconut flakes,
toasted (see note) for garnish

2 limes, quartered

1 Preheat the oven to 300°F. Put the curry in an oven-safe
dish, cover, and heat for 25 to 35 minutes. Heat the couscous
in the same oven, covered, until warmed through, adding a
splash of water to keep the couscous from drying out.

2 Serve the chicken curry in individual bowls over a bed of
couscous, topped with chopped fresh parsley or cilantro and
toasted coconut for some texture and beautiful crunch. Finish
with some freshly squeezed lime juice.

RALLY REMEDIES

• To toast coconut flakes, simply
heat them in a dry large skillet
over medium-low heat, stirring
frequently, until mostly golden
and crisp, 3 to 4 minutes. I
prefer this method for toasting
nuts as well, since I burn them
just about every time I try
toasting them in the oven!

• Serve the curry over cauliflower,
spaghetti squash, lightened-up
pasta, or white beans for a
lighter meal. It's also great
stuffed in a sweet potato if you
want a different way to serve it.

Saucy Meat Stuffed Shells *with* Roasted Squash

SERVES 4

1 Preheat the oven to 350°F. Grease a 9 x 13-inch baking dish with oil.

2 Have the kids help out by stuffing the saucy meat inside each shell and placing them in the baking dish. Once all the shells are stuffed, cover and warm in the oven for 15 to 20 minutes or until warmed through. There will be some meat sauce remaining; heat it in an oven-safe baking dish, covered, to warm through and serve in addition to the stuffed shells. Heat the squash, uncovered, in the same oven in an oven-safe container for 15 minutes, until warm. Serve the shells, extra sauce, and squash together.

RALLY INGREDIENTS

Saucy Meat (page 138)

Pasta Shells (page 139)

Roasted Squash (page 135)

ADDITIONAL INGREDIENTS

Light olive oil, for greasing

RALLY REMEDIES

• You can bring out the unfilled shells and heated meat sauce separately to let everyone assemble and stuff their own at the table for a more interactive meal. To warm up the shells, place in a bowl covered with hot water. Let sit for 5 minutes or so and then strain through a colander.

• This sauce freezes beautifully, so feel free to freeze leftovers. A freezer stash is the greatest gift on hectic days!

CHAPTER 7

Nostalgic Magic

MAKES: 4 DINNERS FOR 4 PEOPLE

This menu is a fun one, loaded with all kid favorites elevated a notch! Green beans and the mushroom-and-onion mixture do double duty in completely different dishes. Anyone else grow up on tuna casserole (or, as we used to call it, "tuna cass")? You're going to love the fun methods used to cook up this flavorful menu.

THIS WEEK'S MENU

- **Sunshine Kebabs** *with* **Hawaij-Spiced Cauliflower**

- **Tuna Cass Hot Dish**

- **"Pisghetti"** *and* **Meat Pillows** *with* **Green Beans**

- **Tortilla Mushroom Egg Bites** *and* **Salad**

PREP

1 **"Pisghetti"** *and* **Elbow Pasta**

2 **Meat Pillows**

3 **Sautéed Mushrooms** *and* **Onions** *and* **Mushroom Cream Sauce**

4 **Green Beans**

5 **Hawaij-Spiced Cauliflower**

6 **Tuna Cass Hot Dish**

7 **Sunshine Kebabs**

NOTES & SWAPS

PREP SMART

- Buy packaged salad kits or greens mix for quick and light side salads.
- Look for haricots verts, a variety of green bean that is thinner and more tender. I always buy green beans with the stems removed to save a tedious step!

PREP IT MORE KID-FRIENDLY

- Serve Sunshine Kebabs in pitas for a more kid-friendly meal. You can also buy some sort of dip for the kebabs to make the meal more fun or make a batch of Green Tahini (page 55).

PREP IT GLUTEN-FREE/LIGHTEN IT UP

- Make the tortilla egg cups without the tortilla and pour the egg mixture right into your muffin tin. Just be sure to use a nonstick muffin tin and grease it super well. I recommend buying silicone muffin liners for this! Alternatively, you can make an omelet or frittata (page 265), adding in the mushrooms and dill.
- Make meat pillows with gluten-free sliced bread.
- Instead of spaghetti use shirataki noodles or zucchini noodles.
- Use gluten-free spaghetti and gluten-free pasta for the Tuna Cass Hot Dish. Replace the flour in the mushroom cream sauce with gluten-free flour.

PREP IT VEGETARIAN

- Substitute Beyond Beef for the meat pillows.
- Replace the Sunshine Kebab chicken with marinated portobello mushrooms, cubed eggplant, or your other favorite vegetables.
- Make the Tuna Cass Hot Dish with white beans, mushrooms, or chickpeas in place of the tuna.

COOKING TOOLS AND EQUIPMENT NEEDED

- Chef's knife
- Cutting board
- 2 (4-quart) saucepans
- 8-quart stockpot
- Colander
- Large bowl
- Small bowls
- Large (12-inch) skillet
- Whisk
- 2 extra-large baking sheets or 3 standard baking sheets
- 9 x 13-inch baking dish
- Storage bag
- Plastic wrap (optional)
- Skewers for kebabs (optional)

GROCERY LIST

PRODUCE

- 2 onions **2** **3**
- 1½ pounds sliced white mushrooms **3**
- 1 big bunch dill **3** **7**
- 48 ounces (3 pounds) green beans **4**
- 36 ounces cauliflower florets or 2 medium heads cauliflower **5**
- 1 lemon **R**
- 1 pomegranate (optional) **R**
- Side salad ingredients for 3 dinners such as lettuce, tomatoes, avocado, carrots, and canned goods (optional) **R**

PANTRY

- Light olive oil
- Cooking oil spray
- Kosher salt
- Pepper
- 3 teaspoons garlic powder **2** **5** **7**
- 1½ teaspoons onion powder **2** **7**
- ½ teaspoon dried oregano **2**
- 1½ teaspoons ground cumin **5**
- 1¼ teaspoons ground turmeric **5** **7**
- 2 tablespoons pure maple syrup **5**
- Pinch of saffron (optional, but highly recommended) **7**
- ⅓ cup low-sodium soy sauce **2**
- ¼ cup balsamic vinegar **2**
- 2 (26-ounce) jars marinara sauce **2**
- 2 tablespoons almond milk or soy milk **2**
- 8 ounces elbow pasta **1**
- 16 ounces spaghetti **1**
- 1 slice sandwich bread **2**
- 3 tablespoons all-purpose flour **3**
- 1 (10-ounce) can tuna in water **6**
- 24 ounces frozen potato tots **6**

- Laffa or pita (optional) **R**
- 6 medium flour tortillas **R**

DAIRY

- 3 tablespoons unsalted butter **3**
- 1½ cups whole milk **3**
- ¼ cup grated Parmesan cheese **6**
- ½ cup cottage cheese **R**
- ½ cup shredded mozzarella cheese **R**

PROTEIN

- 2 pounds ground beef **2**
- 2 pounds chicken breast or thighs (6 breasts or 9 or 10 thighs) **7**
- 1 large egg **2** + 7 eggs **R**

*The "R" symbolizes ingredients you'll be using to Rally throughout the week—these won't be needed in the Sunday prep!

PREP

Time to prep! Set aside about an hour on your Prep day to make these recipes, then store them to use for Rally meals during the week.

1 "Pisghetti" *and* Elbow Pasta

**SERVES 6 AND MAKES 4 SERVINGS PASTA
FOR TUNA CASS HOT DISH**

Kosher salt

16 ounces spaghetti

8 ounces elbow pasta

Light olive oil, for coating

1 Fill two large saucepans halfway with water and salt the water liberally. Bring the water to a boil over high heat. (While you're waiting for the water to boil, get started on the meat pillows on page 157.)

2 Add the spaghetti to one pot and the elbows to the other and cook both according to the package directions until al dente. Drain and rinse the spaghetti, shaking off any excess liquid. Place the spaghetti in a storage container and mix with a drizzle of oil to keep it from sticking together. Cover and store in the fridge. Drain and rinse the elbow noodles and set aside to use in the Tuna Cass later.

2 Meat Pillows

SERVES 6

1 Make the sauce: In a large stockpot, heat the oil over medium-high heat. Add the onion and sauté until softened, 4 to 5 minutes. Add the marinara sauce, balsamic vinegar, and soy sauce and bring to a simmer.

2 Make the meat pillows: In a large bowl, whisk together the egg and almond milk. Sprinkle the bread into the mixture and mash together to fully break up the bread. Add the beef, salt, garlic powder, onion powder, oregano, and pepper. Mix everything just until incorporated.

3 To save time on rolling the meatballs, we're going to make meat pillows with the gnocchi method! Place two long sheets of plastic wrap on the counter. Divide the meat mixture in half and place each in a log in the center of the plastic wrap. Fold both sides of the plastic wrap around the meat, making a long log like how you would make sushi and then twist the ends like a salami to hold it tightly together. Squeeze with your hands to press the meat mixture together in the plastic wrap. Open the plastic and, using a knife, slice the logs into roughly 30 pillows (15 per log), then gently lower them into the sauce. Keep stirring the sauce very gently to submerge all the meat pillows without breaking them. Don't worry if the meatballs don't all submerge right away; as they cook, there will be more liquid in the pot. Just keep (carefully) shaking the pot every 5 to 10 minutes or so, until everything is submerged, then cover and simmer over medium-low heat for 40 to 50 minutes. Let cool completely, then store, covered, in the fridge.

FOR THE SAUCE

2 tablespoons light olive oil

1 medium onion, finely diced

2 (26-ounce) jars marinara sauce

¼ cup balsamic vinegar

⅓ cup low-sodium soy sauce

FOR THE MEAT PILLOWS

1 large egg

2 tablespoons almond milk or soy milk

1 slice sandwich bread, crumbled

2 pounds ground beef

½ teaspoon kosher salt

½ teaspoon garlic powder

½ teaspoon onion powder

½ teaspoon dried oregano

¼ teaspoon pepper

HOT TIPS

• Chop the 2 onions for the meat pillows and mushroom-onion mixture all at once now to save a step later.

• You can of course roll out 30 standard meatballs instead of the gnocchi method if you prefer.

3 Sautéed Mushrooms *and* Onions *and* Mushroom Cream Sauce

MAKES ABOUT 3 CUPS SAUTÉED MUSHROOMS AND ONIONS AND ABOUT 2½ CUPS SAUCE

FOR THE SAUTÉED MUSHROOMS AND ONIONS

1 to 2 tablespoons light olive oil

1 onion, finely diced

1½ pounds sliced white mushrooms, coarsely chopped

Kosher salt and pepper

¼ cup chopped fresh dill

FOR THE MUSHROOM CREAM SAUCE

3 tablespoons unsalted butter

3 tablespoons all-purpose flour

1½ cups whole milk

Kosher salt and pepper

1 Make the sautéed mushroom and onions: In a large skillet, heat the oil over medium-high heat. Add the onion and mushrooms and season with salt and pepper. Sauté for 8 to 10 minutes, until softened. Transfer half (or 1½ cups) of the mushroom-onion mixture to a storage container along with the dill. Cover and store in the fridge for Thursday.

2 Make the mushroom cream sauce: Add the butter to the pan with the remaining half (or 1½ cups) of the mushrooms and onions and let it melt. Add in the flour, then cook, whisking continuously, for 30 seconds or so to cook out the raw flour flavor. Add the milk and whisk so the sauce is completely smooth. Season liberally with salt and pepper and then simmer for 5 minutes, until slightly thickened and creamy. Remove from the heat and set aside for the Tuna Cass assembly.

HOT TIPS

- Wash all the dill now and set aside ½ cup chopped dill for the Sunshine Kebabs (page 160) to save time.

- To make this dish faster, feel free to use the classic canned cream of mushroom soup mix (2½ cups), but the fresher version is much better and healthier!

4 Green Beans

SERVES 8

1 Preheat the oven to 425°F. Line one extra-large baking sheet or two standard baking sheets with parchment paper. Spread the green beans over the prepared pan(s) and season with salt and pepper. Toss with the oil and spread out into a single layer. Roast for 30 to 35 minutes, until cooked through.

2 Chop up 1 cup of the green beans and set aside to use in the Tuna Cass. Let the rest cool, then store, covered, in the fridge.

3 pounds green beans
(48 ounces), tops trimmed as
necessary

Kosher salt and pepper

2 to 3 tablespoons light olive oil

HOT TIP

• Blanch and shock your green beans if you want a more crisp and crunchy result. Fill a large stockpot halfway with water and salt it liberally. Bring to a boil and then add the green beans and cook for 2 to 3 minutes, until the green beans are tender and bright green in color. Meanwhile, fill a large bowl with ice and water. Transfer the green beans to the ice water bath to chill and stop from cooking, then drain and dry them well.

5 Hawaij-Spiced Cauliflower

SERVES 4

Preheat the oven to 425°F. Line a standard baking sheet with parchment paper. Cut the florets into even bite-size pieces. Spread the cauliflower over the baking sheet and toss with the garlic powder, cumin, turmeric, salt and pepper to season, maple syrup, and oil. Roast (ideally on the top rack) for 35 to 40 minutes, until golden and crisp. Let cool, then store, covered, in the fridge.

36 ounces cauliflower florets or
2 medium heads cauliflower

2 teaspoons garlic powder

1½ teaspoons ground cumin

¾ teaspoon ground turmeric

Kosher salt and pepper

2 tablespoons pure maple syrup

3 to 4 tablespoons light olive oil

Sunshine Kebabs *with* Hawaij-Spiced Cauliflower

SERVES 4 TO 6

1 Preheat the oven to 300°F. Heat the cauliflower, uncovered, in an oven-safe storage container until warmed through, about 25 minutes.

2 Remove the chicken from the fridge, add the lemon juice into the bag, seal, and massage to coat.

3 Coat the bottom of a large heavy-bottomed skillet or grill pan with oil and heat over medium-high heat. Remove half the chicken from the marinade with tongs, shaking off as much marinade as possible. Thread the meat onto skewers to make kebabs or add it directly to the pan. Cook until golden on all sides and cooked through, about 10 minutes total. Transfer to a plate and repeat with the remaining chicken.

4 Heat the laffa (if using) in the oven for about 10 minutes to warm up right before eating.

5 Serve the chicken, garnished with freshly chopped dill, together with the cauliflower. Top everything with pomegranate seeds, if desired, and serve with warm laffa.

RALLY INGREDIENTS

Hawaij-Spiced Cauliflower (page 159)

Sunshine Kebabs (page 160)

ADDITIONAL INGREDIENTS

Juice of 1 lemon

Neutral cooking oil for grilling

Laffa or pita, for serving

Extra chopped dill, for garnish (optional)

Pomegranate seeds, for garnish (optional)

RALLY REMEDIES

- Serve this dish in bowls with greens to make the meal lighter.

- I love making these on the grill outside in the summer!

- Switch up this recipe by adding vegetables to the kebabs. Have the kids help prep them too!

CHAPTER 8

Turnip *the* Heat

MAKES: 4 DINNERS FOR 4 PEOPLE

I find it fascinating how influenced we are by our surroundings. Since living in California, I've fallen in love with all the sunny flavors the Golden State has to offer, and poured them into these pages. The recipes may sound complicated or new, but I promise they're super simple and bursting with flavor. This menu is a family favorite in our house!

THIS WEEK'S MENU

- **Mexican-Inspired Chicken Flautas** *with* **Salsa Roja, Guacamole, Cilantro-Lime Rice,** *and* **Turnips**

- **Kufte Smash Burgers** *with* **Pita, Grown-Up Ketchup,** *and* **Cabbage Wedges**

- **DIY Hot Pots**

- **Cheesy Cabbage Bake** *with* **Grown-Up Ketchup**

PREP

1. **Poached Chicken Breasts** *and* **Hot Pot Broth**

2. **Roasted Turnips**

3. **Cabbage Wedges**

4. **Cilantro-Lime Rice**

5. **Salsa Roja**

6. **Kufte Smash Burgers**

7. **Grown-Up Ketchup**

NOTES & SWAPS

PREP SMART

- Save time and buy store-bought salsa and guacamole. It won't be as delicious as these recipes, I can assure you, but it's a great way to shorten your meal prep and save time.

PREP IT MORE KID-FRIENDLY

- You can make the Cheesy Cabbage Bake in individual patties. See page 186 for directions.
- Replace the turnips with russet or sweet potatoes to make more traditional fries.

PREP IT GLUTEN-FREE/LIGHTEN IT UP

- Omit the pitas and just have a burger with cabbage for a lighter dinner.
- Instead of the flautas, make loaded Mexican-style bowls with chicken, lettuce, tomato, rice, corn, guacamole, scallions, cilantro, and Salsa Roja. Serve with turnip fries.

PREP IT VEGETARIAN

- Replace the chicken in the flautas with chopped mushrooms, onions, black beans, and cheese rolled in tortillas. You can also prepare salmon to flake and stuff inside for a pescatarian meal.
- Instead of chicken in the hot pots, you can top your bowls with a 7-minute egg (see page 266) for protein. Add lots of wild mushrooms to the broth to give it a meaty flavor.
- Make the Kufte Smash Burgers with Beyond Beef to make them vegetarian. I omit the salt, as Beyond Beef can be pretty salty on its own.

COOKING TOOLS AND EQUIPMENT NEEDED

- Chef's knife
- Cutting board
- 8-quart stockpot
- 4-quart saucepan
- Fine-mesh sieve
- 1 extra-large baking sheet and 3 standard baking sheets or 4 standard baking sheets
- 1 small bowl
- Immersion blender or high-speed blender
- Microplane
- 32-ounce wide-mouthed jar with lid
- Parchment paper
- Rolling pin or wine bottle
- 4-ounce jar with lid
- 8-ounce storage bowl with lid
- Colander
- Aluminum foil

GROCERY LIST

PRODUCE

- 7 garlic cloves **1** **4** **5**
- 4 ounces baby bella mushrooms **1**
- 1 (2-inch) piece fresh ginger **1**
- 3 medium green cabbages **3**
- 4 large Roma (plum) or vine tomatoes **5**
- 1 onion **5**
- 5 large turnips **2**
- 3 limes **4** **5** **7** + 3 limes R
- 2 bunches parsley or cilantro **1** **4** **5**
- 5 scallions **1** **4** + 6 R
- 2 avocados R
- 2 cups finely shredded napa cabbage R
- 2 cups mung bean sprouts R
- 2 cups thinly sliced carrots R
- 2 cups thinly sliced snap peas R
- 1 small bunch basil R

PANTRY

- Kosher salt
- Pepper
- Light olive oil
- 48 ounces (6 cups) vegetable stock or chicken stock **1**
- 3 tablespoons low-sodium soy sauce **1**
- 1 teaspoon toasted sesame oil **1**
- 1 dried California chile or chipotle pepper in adobo sauce, if preferred (optional) **5**
- 2 cups long-grain brown rice **4**
- ½ cup pine nuts (optional) **4**
- 2 tablespoons sweet paprika **6**
- 2 teaspoons garlic powder **6**
- 1 tablespoon onion powder **6**
- 1 tablespoon ground cumin **6**
- 1 teaspoon curry powder **7**
- ½ cup ketchup **7**
- 2 tablespoons tahini **7**

- 12 to 14 small corn tortillas R
- 4 pitas R
- 1 (15-ounce) can baby corn R
- 8-ounce package ramen or rice noodles R
- Hoisin sauce R
- Hot sauce R
- Red chile flakes R
- Extra-virgin olive oil

DAIRY

- 6 large eggs R
- ¾ cup shredded mozzarella cheese R

PROTEIN

- 6 boneless, skinless chicken breasts **1**
- 1½ pounds ground beef **6**

*The "R" symbolizes ingredients you'll be using to Rally throughout the week—these won't be needed in the Sunday prep!

PREP

Time to prep! Set aside about an hour on your Prep day to make these recipes, then store them to use for Rally meals during the week.

1 Poached Chicken Breasts *and* Hot Pot Broth

SERVES 6 TO 8

6 cups vegetable stock or chicken stock (48 ounces)

3 garlic cloves, smashed and peeled

4 ounces baby bella mushrooms, sliced

1 (2-inch) piece fresh ginger, washed and coarsely chopped (no need to peel)

3 scallions, cut into thirds

1 handful parsley

3 tablespoons low-sodium soy sauce

1 teaspoon toasted sesame oil

Kosher salt and pepper

6 boneless, skinless chicken breasts

1 Place all ingredients except the chicken in a large stockpot and bring to a boil over high heat. Reduce the heat to medium, add the chicken, cover, and simmer for 30 minutes. Transfer the chicken to a bowl.

2 Using a fine-mesh sieve, scoop out all of the solids from the soup so that you have a clear broth. Discard (or see note) all the vegetables—you'll be adding fresh veggies when serving. Shred 3 chicken breasts and return them to the pot. Shred the remaining 3 chicken breasts and transfer to a storage container to use for flautas later in the week.

3 Let everything cool, then cover and store in the fridge.

HOT TIPS

• Instead of throwing out the garlic and mushrooms, pat them dry, roughly chop, and add to the chicken for the flautas. So good! You can also make these into egg rolls using the general directions from Chicken-Broccoli Egg Rolls (page 43) using the chicken, garlic, and mushrooms as the filling.

• Pack leftover hot pots in thermoses for a fun meal on the go!

• Make this soup vegetarian by simply adding lots more mushrooms (including some shiitake and other wild mushrooms) to add flavor.

• If you're making this as a stand-alone recipe, head to page 185 for cooking directions.

2 Roasted Turnips

SERVES 4

1 Preheat the oven to 450°F. Line a standard baking sheet with parchment paper.

2 Quarter the turnips, then cut each quarter in half through the pointed edge to make wedges. Spread them over the baking sheet, coat with oil, and season with salt and pepper. Roast for 50 to 60 minutes, until golden and tender. Let cool, then store, covered, in the fridge.

HOT TIP

• I like leaving the turnips unpeeled for better texture and more crisp!

5 large turnips, scrubbed well

Light olive oil

Kosher salt and pepper

3 Cabbage Wedges

SERVES 8

1 Preheat the oven to 450°F. Line an extra-large baking sheet or two standard baking sheets with parchment paper.

2 Cut each cabbage in quarters, cutting through the core so the wedges stay intact, then cut each quarter in half once more so you have 8 wedges total per cabbage. Place the wedges on the prepared baking sheet(s) and drizzle with the oil. Season liberally with salt and pepper and roast for 50 minutes, or until golden. Remove from the oven, cover immediately with aluminum foil, and set aside to steam for 10 minutes more, to soften and become super tender. Let cool, then store, covered, in the fridge.

3 medium green cabbages, outer leaves peeled and discarded

3 to 4 tablespoons light olive oil

Kosher salt and pepper

Cilantro-Lime Rice

SERVES 8

FOR THE RICE

7 cups water

2 cups long-grain brown rice

Big pinch of kosher salt

FOR THE GREMOLATA

Zest and juice of 1 lime

2 scallions, thinly sliced, then minced

1 garlic clove, minced

Handful of fresh parsley or cilantro, coarsely chopped

2 tablespoons extra-virgin olive oil

Kosher salt and pepper

½ cup pine nuts, toasted (optional)

1 In a medium saucepan, combine the water, rice, and salt. Bring to a boil over high heat, then reduce the heat to maintain a low boil and cook, uncovered, for 30 minutes.

2 Meanwhile, make the gremolata: In a small bowl, whisk together the lime zest and juice, scallions, garlic, parsley, and oil. Season with salt and pepper. Set the gremolata aside.

3 Drain the rice in a colander, but don't rinse it. Return the rice to the pot and add the gremolata. Mix quickly, cover with a lid, and set aside to steam for 10 minutes more. Add the pine nuts now (if using) and then let cool completely. Store, covered, in the fridge.

HOT TIPS

• Gremolata is my secret to making any dish more elegant and flavorful. Make a batch to serve over any roasted vegetable, grilled chicken, seared fish, soup, etc.! Play around with the zests and juices of different citrus fruits and a variety of fresh herbs. It gives food that extra pop of acid and freshness.

• I've been cooking rice for years, and to this day, I still feel like it's so easy to mess up, especially brown rice. My method of boiling it and steaming to finish is foolproof and will ensure your rice is perfectly cooked through every time. Feel free to prepare this recipe with white rice. Cook a batch of basmati rice according to directions on page 197. Mix in the gremolata to finish.

5 Salsa Roja

MAKES ABOUT 2 CUPS

1 Preheat the broiler to high. Make sure an oven rack is in the second-to-highest position. Line a standard baking sheet with aluminum foil or cook directly on the sheet pan.

2 Place the tomatoes, garlic, and onion on the prepared baking sheet in a single layer. Season with salt and pepper and coat with the oil. Broil for 10 minutes, or until you've achieved some blistering and the vegetables have softened. Flip the vegetables over on the sheet pan and continue broiling for an additional 3 to 5 minutes, until cooked through and nicely colored on the other side. If you're using the California chile, add it to the sheet pan in the final minute to toast it ever so slightly, being careful not to burn it.

3 Remove everything from the oven. If you added the California chile, fill a bowl with 2 cups of boiling water and add the freshly toasted chile to submerge. Leave to soften for about 5 minutes before blending.

4 Remove the chile from the water (discard the water) and add the chile and vegetables on the sheet pan to a wide-mouthed storage jar, discarding any juices from the bottom of the baking sheet. Add the lime and cilantro to the jar and blend with an immersion blender until mostly smooth. Taste and season liberally with more salt and pepper as needed. Let cool, then cover and store in the fridge.

4 large Roma (plum) or vine tomatoes, halved

3 garlic cloves, peeled

1 onion, quartered

Kosher salt and pepper

1 to 2 tablespoons light olive oil

1 dried California or dried Anaheim chile, stem trimmed (optional)

Juice of 1 lime (about 2 tablespoons)

½ cup torn fresh cilantro or parsley

HOT TIPS

• Make a double batch of salsa to give you fast and flavorful breakfasts this week. Check out the best chilaquiles (see page 262), or use it as a topping for a frittata (see page 265).

• Never cooked with California chiles? I hadn't either before I moved to California and Silvia (my son Solomon's nanny) introduced me to them. I order them online and love the smoky flavor they give salsa, without any heat! If you want heat, you can add some canned chipotle peppers in adobo sauce before blending the salsa.

6 Kufte Smash Burgers

MAKES 6 BURGERS

1½ pounds ground beef (you can also use ground lamb here)

FOR THE SPICE RUB

2 tablespoons sweet paprika

2 teaspoons garlic powder

1 tablespoon onion powder

1 tablespoon ground cumin

1 tablespoon kosher salt

¼ teaspoon pepper

1 Cut 6 rectangles of parchment paper, about 6 inches wide and the length of the parchment, and fold each in half to make 3-inch squares. Open each parchment square and place the meat between the two layers, portioning out the meat equally. Don't overwork the meat—just place it freeform. Cover the top layer of parchment over and press down to flatten, rolling each one with a rolling pin or wine bottle (use what you got). These will be extra-crispy burgers with lots of surface area for crunchy edges. Place everything, lying flat, in a large storage bag in the fridge to cook fresh later in the week.

2 Make the spice blend: Combine all the spices in a small jar, cover, and leave on the counter.

HOT TIPS

- No time for rolling out burgers between parchment? Form traditional burgers, and smash them directly in the pan with a spatula when frying to achieve a similar effect.

- If you're making this as a stand-alone recipe, head to page 182 for cooking directions.

7 Grown-Up Ketchup

MAKES ABOUT ¾ CUP

½ cup ketchup

2 tablespoons tahini

1 teaspoon curry powder

½ teaspoon kosher salt

Juice of 1 lime (about 2 tablespoons)

2 teaspoons water, plus more as needed

Whisk together all the ingredients in a storage jar, adding more water as needed to thin the mixture. Cover and store in the fridge.

RALLY

Get ready to Rally! Time to take all those
Prep staples and use them to
create delicious meals for the week.

Kufte Smash Burgers *with* Pita, Grown-Up Ketchup, *and* Cabbage Wedges

SERVES 4 TO 6

RALLY INGREDIENTS

Cabbage Wedges (page 175; reserve 4 cups for Thursday)

Uncooked Kufte Smash Burgers and spice rub (page 178)

½ recipe Grown-Up Ketchup (page 178)

ADDITIONAL INGREDIENTS

4 pitas

Neutral oil, for frying

1 Preheat the oven to 300°F. Chop up 4 cups of cabbage and reserve in the fridge for the Cheesy Cabbage Bake (page 186). Heat the remaining cabbage, uncovered, in an oven-safe baking dish for about 15 minutes, until warmed through. Heat the pitas directly on the oven rack in the same oven for 6 to 7 minutes, until warmed.

2 Meanwhile, in a large skillet, heat 1 tablespoon oil over medium-high heat. Peel off the top layer of parchment paper from one of the burgers and sprinkle the top of the burger with ¾ teaspoon of the spice rub. Flip the burger into the hot pan, spiced side down, and remove the parchment completely. Sprinkle the top of the burger with another ¾ teaspoon of the spice rub. Fry for 3 minutes or so on the first side, until crisp and golden, then flip and cook on the other side for 2 to 3 minutes more. Transfer to a plate and repeat to cook the remaining burgers. Wipe out the pan halfway through and add more oil as needed.

3 Serve the burgers with the cabbage and warm pitas, topped with the grown-up ketchup.

RALLY REMEDIES

- Serve these in buns with ketchup and mustard, more like traditional burgers, if the kids prefer.

- I love serving these at a BBQ, but when I do, I keep the burgers a little thicker so they don't fall apart on the grill.

DIY Hot Pots

SERVES 4 TO 6

1 Cook the ramen or rice noodles according to package directions in a small saucepan. Rinse, drain, and place into a serving bowl.

2 Meanwhile, put the chicken and hot pot broth in a large stockpot and bring to a boil over medium-high heat.

3 Place the add-ins of your choosing in separate little bowls and display them on the table along with the noodles.

4 Have everyone fill their own bowl with their favorite add-ins and then pour the piping-hot broth (with chicken) over. Garnish as desired and enjoy.

RALLY INGREDIENTS

Hot Pot Broth with Poached Chicken (page 174)

ADDITIONAL INGREDIENTS

8 ounces ramen or rice noodles

Hoisin sauce

1 (15-ounce) can baby corn, drained and chopped

2 cups finely shredded napa cabbage

2 cups mung bean sprouts

2 cups thinly sliced carrots

2 cups thinly sliced snap peas

3 scallions, thinly sliced

Hot sauce

Red chile flakes

2 limes, cut into wedges

1 small bunch basil

1 small bunch cilantro

RALLY REMEDIES

• To serve this differently, you can decide which add-ins work for your family and cook the vegetables in the broth right before serving. Let everyone add their own garnishes at the table.

• If you happen to have a portable burner and want to serve this my favorite way, you can bring the pot of broth to the table (or even dine alfresco) and cook it tableside with your family or friends. It's a fun way to entertain.

Cheesy Cabbage Bake *with* Grown-Up Ketchup

SERVES 4 TO 6

RALLY INGREDIENTS

Cabbage Wedges (reserved from page 182), chopped (4 cups)

½ recipe Grown-Up Ketchup (page 178)

ADDITIONAL INGREDIENTS

Light olive oil or cooking oil spray, for greasing

6 large eggs

¾ cup shredded mozzarella cheese

3 scallions, thinly sliced

1¼ teaspoons kosher salt

¼ teaspoon pepper

Salad ingredients of your choosing (optional)

1 Preheat the oven to 400°F. Grease a 9 x 13-inch baking dish with oil.

2 In a large bowl, mix together the cabbage, eggs, mozzarella, scallions, salt, and pepper. Pour into the prepared baking dish and bake for 40 minutes, or until set and golden.

3 Serve with the grown-up ketchup. Assemble a salad to complete the meal, if desired.

RALLY REMEDIES

• If you prefer to make this into individual fritters rather than baking it in one dish, simply mix ¼ cup all-purpose flour into the batter and fry the patties in a nonstick skillet until golden on both sides, 3 to 4 minutes per side. It's a faster way to get dinner on the table!

• To serve this a different way, make a batch of rice and then make a version of fried rice (page 268), adding in chopped-up cabbage, soy sauce, toasted sesame oil, and scrambled eggs.

CHAPTER 9

One-Pan Heroes

MAKES: 4 DINNERS FOR 4 PEOPLE

You know by now that I'm all about the interactive dinners and getting the kids involved in the process. Cooking can be loads of fun for kids, and it truly helps to create better eaters. If you have the week scheduled out and shopped for, it's less stressful letting them help. This menu gives you lots of great opportunities to call on the kiddos for assistance with tasks like rolling enchiladas, shredding meat, prepping salads/vegetable prep, blending salsa, and mixing sauces. I've also come up with a sesame noodle recipe that's a true one-pot meal and sure to please everyone. Andi and Jolie gave both thumbs and "toe thumbs" up, and if you follow my Instagram stories you know that means something was good!

- **Barbacoa Tacos** *with* **Slaw, Avocado,** *and* **Rice**

- **Sesame Noodle Chicken Bake** *and*
  Cucumber Salad

- **Green Enchiladas** *with* **Salsa Verde** *and* **Slaw**

- **Sabich Bar**

PREP

1 **Barbacoa**

2 **Eggplant**

3 **Sesame Noodle Chicken Bake**

4 **Rice**

5 **Salsa Verde**

6 **Slaw**

7 **Enchilada Assembly**

NOTES & SWAPS

PREP SMART

- Don't want to spend the money on brisket? Spice up a flank steak, oyster steak, or skirt steak and grill or sear. Serve it sliced in tacos for a less expensive option.
- Able to buy a great salsa verde in your grocery store and want save time prepping this week? More power to you! If you want to make your own salsa and can't find tomatillos, you can replace them with 1 green bell pepper (or 2 poblano peppers) and 3 Roma (plum) tomatoes. See page 198 for directions.
- If you don't want tacos, buy burger buns and have pulled beef sandwiches with slaw.

PREP IT MORE KID-FRIENDLY

- If your kids are scared of the salsa verde, feel free to make some without the sauce or use marinara sauce in its place.
- Instead of the enchiladas, fry up some quesadillas by sandwiching the rice, beans, and cheese between two tortillas and pan-frying to cook. Serve dunked in the salsa verde.
- Make a batch of store-bought oven fries for the sabich bar. The kids will love adding them to their sandwiches or bowls.

PREP IT GLUTEN-FREE/LIGHTEN IT UP

- Use almond tortillas or cassava tortillas instead of wheat tortillas for the enchiladas and barbacoa tacos. You can even serve the barbacoa in lettuce cups.
- Marinate boneless, skinless chicken cutlets in the sesame-soy mixture for 30 minutes and grill. Serve with cucumber salad and cooked rice noodles or zucchini noodles on the side, if desired.

PREP IT VEGETARIAN

- Instead of the barbacoa, serve tacos loaded with refried beans (I love Amy's brand canned refried beans), Chili-Spiced Sweet Potatoes (page 33), slaw, and guacamole. Serve with cilantro, jalapeños, sour cream, and lime. You can also use jackfruit in place of the pulled beef.
- The chicken bake is great with tofu instead! See page 197 for details. You can also pan-fry your favorite chopped vegetables instead of the chicken. Mushrooms, peppers, and Broccolini along with the onion and garlic are great.

COOKING TOOLS AND EQUIPMENT NEEDED

- Chef's knife
- Cutting board
- Heavy-bottomed medium (6-quart) stockpot or Dutch oven with lid
- Tongs
- Vegetable peeler
- 1 extra-large baking sheet and 1 standard baking sheet or 3 standard baking sheets
- Small bowl
- 10-inch sauté pan
- Large plate
- Fine-mesh sieve
- 4-quart saucepan with lid
- Immersion blender or high-speed blender
- 32-ounce wide-mouthed storage jar with lid
- Large storage bowl with lid
- 16-ounce wide-mouthed storage jar with lid
- 9 x 13-inch baking dish

1 Barbacoa

SERVES 4

1 (2-pound) second-cut brisket, cut into 3 equal portions (for faster cooking)

Kosher salt and pepper

1 tablespoon ground cumin

1 tablespoon mild chili powder

1 teaspoon garlic powder

1 teaspoon dried oregano

2 tablespoons light olive oil

½ onion, thinly sliced (save the other half for the Sesame Noodle Chicken Bake)

4 garlic cloves, peeled and coarsely chopped

1 tablespoon tomato paste

1 cup vegetable stock or beef stock

1 bay leaf

¼ cup apple cider vinegar

1 Season the brisket with salt and pepper on all sides, then coat with the cumin, chili powder, garlic powder, and oregano. Massage to coat in the spices.

2 In a heavy-bottomed medium stockpot or Dutch oven, heat the oil over high heat. Working in batches as needed, sear the brisket for 4 to 5 minutes per side to form a golden crust. Add the onion and garlic and mix together with the chunks of meat. Cook for 2 to 3 minutes to caramelize, then stir in the tomato paste and cook for another minute. Add the stock, bay leaf, and vinegar and bring to a boil. Reduce the heat to maintain a simmer, cover, and cook for 2½ to 3 hours, flipping the brisket pieces once halfway through, until tender.

3 Transfer the brisket to a storage container and shred the meat using two forks. Discard the bay leaf and pour half the sauce and all the onion over the brisket; discard the remaining sauce. Let cool completely, then cover and store in the fridge.

HOT TIPS

• You can also prep all the ingredients in a slow cooker insert and store it in the fridge. The day you plan to serve it, set the insert in the slow cooker, cover, and cook on Low for 6 to 7 hours. There's no need to sear the meat here if you want to skip it. You can also cook this in the oven at 300°F for 2 to 3 hours, or in an Instant Pot for a faster braise.

• Cook the brisket whole (instead of cutting it into thirds) if you want to serve it sliced for another occasion or use. Sear it in a pan, then transfer to a baking dish and add the remaining ingredients. Cook closer to the 3-hour mark to ensure it's super soft and tender.

• You can replace the brisket with a quick-cooking cut of steak such as London broil or skirt steak. Use a 2-pound steak and simply coat it in the spices, omitting everything else. Grill or sear in a large pan for 5 to 6 minutes on each side. Slice the steak into thin strips prior to serving in tacos.

• To make this vegetarian, use jackfruit and cook it using the same general directions as the brisket but cooking for only 30 minutes.

2 Eggplant

SERVES 4

1 Preheat the oven to 450°F. Line an extra-large baking sheet or two standard baking sheets with parchment paper.

2 Trim the tops and bottoms off each eggplant. Using a vegetable peeler, peel off random strips of skin, peeling lengthwise to give each eggplant stripes (I keep some skin on so the eggplant doesn't completely fall apart when it cooks). Cut each eggplant in half lengthwise, then slice crosswise into ½-inch-thick half-moons. Place the eggplant on the prepared baking sheet(s), arranging the slices in a single layer as best you can. Sprinkle some salt on both sides and then coat liberally with oil. Roast on the top rack for 35 to 40 minutes, flipping the pieces halfway through so they brown evenly. If you're using two baking sheets, swap their positions halfway through so each has time on the top rack. Let cool, then store, covered, in the fridge.

3 medium eggplants

Kosher salt

3 to 4 tablespoons light olive oil

HOT TIP

- If you prefer to fry the eggplant in a skillet, place the eggplant pieces on a clean kitchen towel and season both sides with salt. Let sit for 10 minutes undisturbed. Then, using another towel, press down on the eggplant pieces to remove some excess moisture. Fill a rimmed pan with 1 to 2 tablespoons of neutral cooking oil and heat over high heat. Working in batches, fry the eggplant in the hot oil until deeply golden on both sides. Transfer to a paper towel–lined plate and continue with the rest. I prefer the frying method when I'm cooking them fresh right before eating.

3 Sesame Noodle Chicken Bake

SERVES 4

⅓ cup low-sodium soy sauce

3 tablespoons rice vinegar

2 tablespoons toasted sesame oil

2 tablespoons pure maple syrup

1¾ cups water

2 tablespoons light olive oil

1 whole chicken, cut up

Kosher salt and pepper

½ onion, thinly sliced (reserved from the barbacoa on page 194)

3 garlic cloves, minced

8 ounces white spaghetti, cracked into thirds

1 Preheat the oven to 450°F.

2 In a small bowl, whisk together the soy sauce, vinegar, sesame oil, maple syrup, and water. Set aside.

3 In a high-sided large oven-safe sauté pan or Dutch oven, heat the oil over high heat. Season the chicken pieces on both sides (and under the skin as best as possible) with salt and pepper and place skin side down in the pan. Cook until deeply golden, about 5 minutes, then flip and sear on the second side for 3 to 4 minutes, until golden. Transfer all the chicken to a plate (it will only be partially cooked at this point; that's okay). Add the onion and garlic and cook for 3 to 4 minutes, until softened. Reduce the heat to medium and add the soy mixture, stirring and scraping up all the bits from the bottom of the pan.

4 Add the cracked spaghetti and mix to submerge all the noodles in the liquid. Place the chicken on top, skin side down. Bring to a boil over high heat, then immediately cover with a tight-fitting lid or aluminum foil and bake, covered, in the oven for 15 minutes. Pull the oven rack out halfway and uncover the pan. Flip the chicken so the pieces are now skin side up, and give the spaghetti a little mix underneath. Slide the oven rack back in and bake, uncovered, for an additional 15 minutes until the chicken is golden and all the liquid has mostly absorbed. Feel free to broil for the last few minutes to brown even more. Let cool, then store, covered, in the fridge.

4 Rice

SERVES 8

In a large saucepan, combine the water and a big pinch of salt and bring to a boil over high heat. Rinse the rice with cold water through a fine-mesh sieve until the water runs clear. Shake to drain off any excess liquid. Add the rice to the boiling water and bring back to a boil. Immediately reduce the heat to maintain a simmer and cover with a tight-fitting lid. Simmer for 15 minutes. Remove from the heat and set aside, covered, to allow the rice to steam for 10 minutes more. Set aside 1½ cups of the rice for the enchiladas. Let the rest cool, then store, covered, in the fridge.

3½ cups water

Kosher salt

2 cups long-grain white basmati rice

HOT TIPS

• To make this vegetarian, use 1 (16-ounce) block extra-firm tofu in place of the chicken. Cut the tofu into 1-inch cubes and dry them well on a clean kitchen towel. Season liberally with salt and pepper. In a large nonstick skillet, heat 2 to 3 tablespoons oil over high heat and fry until crisp and golden. Transfer to a plate and then continue with the recipe as directed. You can also add in your favorite frozen veggies to make it even more vegetarian friendly.

• You can make this recipe with whole-wheat spaghetti instead, but my kids prefer it with white. Pick your battles. ☺

• To make this a lighter meal, marinate chicken cutlets in the sesame-soy mixture, omitting the water and adding the minced garlic to the marinade. Let marinate for 30 minutes or up to an hour and then grill the chicken.

5 Salsa Verde

MAKES ABOUT 3 CUPS

2 onions, quartered

6 garlic cloves, peeled

10 large tomatillos, husks
   removed, and halved

1 jalapeño, stemmed, halved
   lengthwise, and seeded
   (optional)

3 tablespoons light olive oil

Kosher salt and pepper

½ teaspoon dried oregano

Juice of 2 limes

1 cup fresh cilantro or parsley,
   roughly torn

1 Preheat the broiler to high (make sure an oven rack is in the second-to-highest position). Line a standard baking sheet with aluminum foil or place ingredients directly on the sheet pan. Put the onions, garlic, tomatillos, and jalapeño (if using) on the baking sheet. Coat with the oil and season with salt and pepper. Spread the vegetables out in an even layer to ensure nothing touches the broiler itself. Broil for 10 minutes, or until charred, then flip (breaking up the onions a bit) and broil for an additional 5 minutes, until nicely browned and charred in some places on the second side. Keep a close eye on the broiler to ensure everything is safely charring!

2 Transfer the vegetables and any pan juices to a wide-mouthed storage container (or a high-powered blender) and add the oregano, lime juice, and cilantro. Blend with an immersion blender until mostly smooth. Taste and season with more salt and pepper until well seasoned. Let cool, then set aside to use for the enchiladas later.

HOT TIP

- No tomatillos? Replace them with 1 large green bell pepper (or 2 poblano peppers), seeded and roughly chopped, and 3 Roma (plum) tomatoes, halved. Add to the baking sheet along with the onions, garlic, and optional jalapeño and continue with the recipe as directed.

6 Slaw

SERVES 6 (MAKES ABOUT 1 CUP SAUCE)

1 Make the slaw: Combine all the slaw ingredients in a large bowl and store, covered, in the fridge.

2 Make the mayo-less slaw sauce: Combine all the sauce ingredients in a jar, cover, and shake to mix. Taste for seasoning and add more salt and pepper as needed. Store in the fridge.

FOR THE SLAW

1 medium head purple cabbage, halved, cored, and thinly shaved or about 2 (16-ounce) bags slaw mix

3 celery stalks, finely diced (about 2 cups)

3 scallions, thinly sliced

FOR THE MAYO-LESS SLAW SAUCE

½ cup rice vinegar

⅓ cup extra-virgin olive oil

1 teaspoon ground coriander

1 tablespoon Dijon mustard

1 tablespoon pure maple syrup

Kosher salt and pepper

HOT TIP

• I've never liked a thick, mayo-based coleslaw, which is why I'm sharing my favorite acidic vinaigrette, or as I call it, "mayo-less slaw sauce." I think it's the only way slaw should be served, but if you're a mayo fan, feel free to add ¼ to ½ cup mayonnaise for a more traditional slaw dressing.

7 Enchilada Assembly

SERVES 4 TO 6

Light olive oil or cooking oil spray, for greasing

2½ cups Salsa Verde (page 198)

1½ cups Rice (page 197)

1 (15.5-ounce) can black beans, drained and rinsed

2 cups shredded mozzarella cheese

1 teaspoon onion powder

½ teaspoon garlic powder

Kosher salt and pepper

6 medium flour tortillas

1 Grease a 9 x 13-inch baking dish with oil. Pour in ½ cup of the salsa verde, spreading it to coat the bottom of the dish.

2 In a large bowl, combine the rice, black beans, 1 cup of the salsa verde, and 1 cup of the mozzarella and mix together. Season with the onion powder, garlic powder, and a pinch each of salt and pepper.

3 Working with one tortilla at a time, place about ½ cup of the filling in the center of each tortilla and roll them into cylinders. Place them seam side down in the baking dish.

4 Spread 1 more cup of the salsa verde over the tops of the enchiladas and finish with the remaining 1 cup mozzarella to top. Reserve and store any leftover salsa from your Prep for serving with the enchiladas later in the week. Cover tightly and store in the fridge.

HOT TIPS

• If you want to skip a step on Sunday, you can prep the enchilada ingredients and roll them fresh prior to cooking later in the week.

• Try layering the filling ingredients like a lasagna instead of rolling up the tortillas to save time.

• If you're making this as a stand-alone recipe, head to page 207 for cooking directions.

RALLY

Get ready to Rally! Time to take all those
Prep staples and use them to
create delicious meals for the week.

Barbacoa Tacos *with* Slaw, Avocado, *and* Rice

SERVES 4

1 Preheat the oven to 300°F. Heat the barbacoa, covered, in an oven-safe storage container for 30 minutes, or until warmed through. Add a splash of water to the rice and heat, covered, in the same oven, in an oven-safe container for 25 to 30 minutes.

2 Toss the slaw with the slaw sauce and season with additional salt as needed. Serve the barbacoa in the taco shells, loaded with the rice, slaw, and sliced avocado.

RALLY INGREDIENTS

Barbacoa (page 194)

Rice (page 197)

½ recipe Slaw (page 199)

ADDITIONAL INGREDIENTS

6 to 8 hard taco shells

2 avocados, sliced

RALLY REMEDY

- Feel free to swap out the hard taco shells for soft tortillas. I love using almond tortillas and charring them over an open flame prior to serving. The barbacoa is even delicious in lettuce cups for a lighter dinner.

Sesame Noodle Chicken Bake *and* Cucumber Salad

<u>SERVES 4</u>

RALLY INGREDIENTS

Sesame Noodle Chicken Bake (page 196)

ADDITIONAL INGREDIENTS

2 English cucumbers

3 tablespoons rice vinegar

Pinch of sugar (optional)

1 to 2 tablespoons light olive oil

Kosher salt and pepper

1 to 2 tablespoons toasted sesame seeds

2 scallions, thinly sliced

Red chile flakes (optional)

1 Preheat the oven to 300°F. Add a splash of water to the sesame noodle chicken bake and heat, covered, in an oven-safe dish for 25 to 30 minutes, until heated through. (The water helps keep it from drying out.)

2 Meanwhile, halve the cucumbers lengthwise and then slice crosswise into half-moons. Put the cucumbers in a large bowl and add the vinegar, sugar, oil, and salt and pepper to taste, for a fresh and super-kid-friendly side dish.

3 Top the sesame noodle chicken bake with the sesame seeds and scallions, and garnish with chile flakes, if you like. Serve the cucumber salad on the side.

RALLY REMEDY

- Shred or chop up the chicken to mix into the sesame noodles. Alternatively, serve the chicken on the bone alongside the sesame noodles.

Green Enchiladas *with* Salsa Verde *and* Slaw

SERVES 4

1 Preheat the oven to 375°F. Remove the enchiladas from the fridge and bake, covered, for 30 minutes. Uncover the baking dish and cook for 15 minutes more, or until the cheese is bubbling and golden. Meanwhile, place the slaw in a bowl and toss with the slaw sauce. Season with salt and pepper as needed.

2 Serve the enchiladas immediately, topped with the sour cream and onion and fresh limes, leftover salsa (if using), and the slaw on the side.

RALLY INGREDIENTS

Uncooked Green Enchiladas (page 200)

½ recipe Slaw (page 199)

Salsa Verde (page 198), for serving (optional)

ADDITIONAL INGREDIENTS

Kosher salt and pepper

1½ cups sour cream, for topping

½ red onion, finely diced

2 limes, cut into wedges, for serving

RALLY REMEDIES

• Save the other half of the red onion for the sabich bar.

• Make quesadillas with the rice, beans, and cheese, if you prefer those to enchiladas. Dunk in sour cream and salsa verde. Use any kind of tortilla you love for a lighter meal.

Sabich Bar

SERVES 4

RALLY INGREDIENTS

Eggplant (page 195)

ADDITIONAL INGREDIENTS

6 large eggs

Kosher salt

FOR THE ISRAELI SALAD

2 English cucumbers, finely diced

4 ripe Roma (plum) tomatoes, finely diced

½ red onion, finely diced

1 (19-ounce) can Israeli pickles in brine, finely diced

Leftover fresh parsley or cilantro, chopped

Juice of 1 lemon

3 tablespoons extra-virgin olive oil

Kosher salt and pepper

TOPPINGS

Store-bought seasoned tahini (I like the kind that comes in a squeeze bottle)

Store-bought amba (optional)

Hot sauce or harissa

1 cup labneh or crumbled feta cheese

1 (6- to 8-ounce) bag pita chips or 4 pitas, to make into chips or serve fresh

1 Preheat the oven to 400°F. Spread the eggplant out on a parchment-lined baking sheet and warm for 10 minutes or so. If you have an air fryer, feel free to warm and crisp up the eggplant in there. (If you want to fry the eggplant fresh, do so now following directions on page 195.)

2 Meanwhile, fill a medium pot halfway with water, season generously with salt, and bring to a boil over high heat. Fill a bowl with ice and water and set it nearby. When the water comes to a boil, carefully drop in the eggs and boil for exactly 7 minutes for a jammy soft-boiled egg or 9 minutes for a more hard-boiled one. Remove from the pot with a slotted spoon and plunge into the ice-water bath to stop the eggs from cooking and cool. Peel and set aside. (You can fry the eggs instead, if you prefer!)

3 Make the Israeli salad: In a medium bowl, combine the cucumbers, tomatoes, onion, pickles, and parsley. Add the lemon juice and olive oil, toss to coat, and season liberally with salt and pepper.

4 Place the toppings in individual small bowls. Set up the sabich bar, displaying all the fixins and letting everyone build their own bowls or make sabich sandwiches by stuffing the ingredients into pitas. Serve topped with the labneh or feta.

RALLY REMEDIES

• Making your own pita chips is super easy, and a great way to repurpose stale pitas. Cut each pita into triangles and toss on a baking sheet with oil and salt (or experiment with other spices!). Bake at 400°F for 7 to 10 minutes, until golden brown and crisp.

• I love making sabich nachos! Spread your pita chips over a baking sheet and top with all the fixins. No need to cook, of course, as everything is ready to go. Serve family-style and let everyone dig in.

• Make some store-bought freezer fries to go along with this meal.

CHAPTER 10

Sun's Out, Buns Out

MAKES: 4 DINNERS FOR 4 PEOPLE

This menu just feels like summer to me. We've become so obsessed with pizza in our house since I bought my husband, Mike, a pizza oven for his birthday this past year. If we even mention the word "pizza," Solomon sprints outside and starts yelling "Patzie! Patzie!" We reserve pizza for weekends, since manning a wood-burning pizza oven is truly a two-person job, but I've created the best alternative for those busier nights: my Balsamic Onion Sheet Pan Pizza (page 228). Add any toppings your family loves or even dedicate rows for each person to customize their own. The rest of the menu is pretty stellar too—if I may say so myself—as it includes many kid favorites and repeat-worthy dinners.

GROCERY LIST

PRODUCE

- 4 large onions ①
- 2 pounds asparagus ③
- 6 ears corn ④
- 1 lemon ⑦ + 1 lemon R
- 1 lime ⑦ R
- 3 garlic cloves ⑦
- 1 head Bibb lettuce R
- 1 large ripe tomato R
- 1 bunch basil (optional) R
- 1 bunch cilantro (optional) R
- Arugula (optional) R

PANTRY

- Kosher salt
- Pepper
- Light olive oil
- Neutral cooking oil
- Cooking oil spray
- ½ cup balsamic vinegar ①
- 3 tablespoons pure maple syrup ① ⑤
- 2 cups quinoa ②
- 1 teaspoon garlic powder ⑤
- 1 tablespoon plus 1 teaspoon low-sodium soy sauce ⑤
- ½ cup ketchup ⑤
- 2½ cups panko bread crumbs ⑤ ⑥
- 1 teaspoon sweet paprika ⑥
- 1 teaspoon onion powder ⑥
- ½ cup coarse cornmeal or grits ⑥
- ¼ cup all-purpose flour ⑥
- ¾ teaspoon mild chili powder ⑦
- ½ cup plus 2 tablespoons mayonnaise ⑧
- 1 tablespoon rice vinegar ⑧
- 2 tablespoons honey ⑧
- 2 tablespoons Dijon mustard ⑧

- Red chile flakes or sliced Calabrian chiles (optional) R
- 2 pounds store-bought pizza dough R
- All-purpose flour R
- 4 to 6 ciabatta or burger buns R
- 1 jar of your favorite pickles
- Cholula or Frank's RedHot hot sauce R (optional)

PROTEIN

- 1½ pounds ground chicken ⑤
- 2 pounds boneless, skinless chicken breasts ⑥
- 4 (6-ounce) skinless bass fillets (halibut or cod work well too) ⑦

DAIRY AND EGGS

- 4 large eggs ⑤ ⑥
- ½ cup (1 stick) unsalted butter ⑦
- 1 cup crumbled feta, Parmesan, or Cotija cheese (optional) R
- 2½ cups shredded mozzarella cheese R

*The "R" symbolizes ingredients you'll be using to Rally throughout the week—these won't be needed in the Sunday prep!

PREP

Time to prep! Set aside about an hour on your Prep day to make these recipes, then store them to use for Rally meals during the week.

1 Balsamic Jammy Onions

MAKES ABOUT 2 CUPS

2 tablespoons light olive oil

4 large onions, halved and thinly sliced

½ teaspoon kosher salt

½ cup balsamic vinegar

2 tablespoons pure maple syrup

1 In a large skillet, heat the oil over medium-high heat. Add the onions and the salt and cook, stirring, for about 10 minutes, until nicely broken down and golden. Reduce the heat to medium and carefully add the vinegar and maple syrup. Cook for 15 minutes, or until the liquid has mostly been absorbed and the onions are super soft and sticky.

2 Transfer ½ cup of the onions to a large bowl (you'll be making the meatloaf in this bowl) and set aside. Let the rest cool, then store, covered, in the fridge.

2 Basic Quinoa

SERVES 6

2 cups quinoa

3½ cups water

Pinch of kosher salt

1 In a medium saucepan, combine the quinoa and water and bring to a boil over high heat. Reduce the heat to maintain a simmer, cover, and cook for 10 minutes, or until all the liquid has been absorbed.

2 Measure ½ cup of the quinoa and add it to the bowl with the jammy onions that you'll be using for the meatloaf. Transfer the rest of the quinoa to a storage container and let cool, then cover and store in the fridge.

HOT TIPS

- If you're making quick-cooking couscous, cook the same amount as the quinoa, following package directions.

- You will end up with some leftover quinoa this week, but I honestly consider that a blessing, as it's the perfect base for just about any meal. Make yourself a nice grain bowl for lunch, Leftover Grains Porridge (page 243) for breakfast, or place leftovers on a baking sheet coated in some oil and bake at 350°F for 30 to 40 minutes until crisp. Use it to top salads, yogurts, or anything else you want to add crunch and protein to. If you'd rather not have so much, cut the recipe in half.

3 Asparagus

SERVES 4

Preheat the oven to 375°F. Line a standard baking sheet with parchment paper. Spread the asparagus over the baking sheet, coat with the oil, and season with salt and pepper. Roast for 12 to 15 minutes, until bright green and just cooked. Let cool, then store, covered, in the fridge.

2 pounds asparagus, bottoms trimmed

2 to 3 tablespoons light olive oil

Kosher salt and pepper

4 Corn

SERVES 4 TO 6

Preheat the oven to 375°F. Place the corn in a baking dish or on a standard baking sheet lined with parchment paper. Massage the oil over the corn and season with some salt. Roast for 25 minutes, or until just cooked through. You will be broiling these fresh with butter sauce prior to serving, so don't overcook them now. Let cool, then store, covered, in the fridge.

6 ears corn, husks removed

2 tablespoons light olive oil

Kosher salt

HOT TIP

• If you're making this as a stand-alone recipe and want to make it street-corn-style simple, prep half the Citrus Butter (see page 220), then head to page 223 for cooking directions.

5 Meatloaf

SERVES 4 TO 6

FOR THE MEATLOAF

½ cup cooked Quinoa (page 216)

½ cup Balsamic Jammy Onions (page 216)

1½ pounds ground chicken

¼ cup ketchup

2 large eggs

1 tablespoon low-sodium soy sauce

½ cup panko bread crumbs

1 teaspoon kosher salt

1 teaspoon garlic powder

FOR THE GLAZE

1 teaspoon low-sodium soy sauce

¼ cup ketchup

1 tablespoon pure maple syrup

1 Preheat the oven to 375°F.

2 Make the meatloaf: Line a standard baking sheet with parchment paper.

3 To the bowl with the quinoa and onions, add the ground chicken, ketchup, eggs, soy sauce, panko, salt, and garlic powder and mix just until combined. Turn the meat mixture out onto the prepared baking sheet and form it into a rectangle roughly 6 x 11 inches in size. Bake for 20 minutes.

4 Meanwhile, make the glaze: In a small bowl, whisk together the soy sauce, ketchup, and maple syrup.

5 Pull the meatloaf halfway out of the oven and brush with all the glaze, then bake for 20 to 25 minutes more, until the meatloaf is firm and the glaze on top is sticky. Let cool, then store, covered, in the fridge.

HOT TIPS

- You can also make these into individual burgers or mini meatloaves.

- Add some grated vegetables and/or fresh herbs to make this meatloaf even heartier, or use Beyond Beef to make it vegetarian. Add extra flavor pops such as chopped sun-dried tomatoes, olives, etc.!

- Feel free to use prepared rice instead of quinoa.

6 Crispy Chicken Katsu

SERVES 4

1 Cut each thinly sliced chicken breast in half and set aside. In a large storage bag, combine the panko, cornmeal, paprika, onion powder, and ¾ teaspoon of the salt. Seal the bag, shake to mix, and store on the counter for later in the week.

2 Crack the eggs into another large storage bag and add the water, flour, and remaining ¾ teaspoon salt. Massage to mix well. Add the chicken to the bag with the egg mixture, seal, and massage to coat every piece of chicken in the batter. Store in the fridge for later in the week. You'll be coating the chicken in the panko mixture and cooking it fresh just before serving. Or, to cook it now, skip ahead to page 224.

2 pounds boneless, skinless chicken breasts, thinly cut in half

2 cups panko bread crumbs

½ cup coarse cornmeal or grits

1 teaspoon sweet paprika

1 teaspoon onion powder

1½ teaspoons kosher salt, divided

2 large eggs

2 tablespoons water

¼ cup all-purpose flour

HOT TIPS

• To make this a vegetarian katsu, use eggplant! Cut the tops and bottoms off 2 small eggplants and slice them lengthwise into ½-inch-thick planks (you should end up with 8 to 9 planks total). Coat each eggplant with a thin layer of egg mixture and then dredge in the panko. Bake or fry as you would the chicken.

• If you're making this as a stand-alone recipe, head to page 224 for cooking directions.

7 Citrus Butter Bass

SERVES 4 (MAKES ½ CUP CITRUS BUTTER)

4 (6-ounce) skinless sea bass fillets (halibut or cod work well too), bones removed

Kosher salt and pepper

FOR THE CITRUS BUTTER

½ cup (1 stick) unsalted butter, at room temperature

3 garlic cloves, minced

¾ teaspoon mild chili powder

Zest of 1 lime (reserving the rest of the lime for serving later in the week)

Pinch of salt

1 lemon, sliced into 6 rounds, for serving

1 Place the fish in a baking dish large enough to fit the fillets without crowding. Season the tops liberally with salt and pepper.

2 Make the citrus butter: Place the softened butter in a small bowl and whisk in the garlic, chili powder, lime zest (store the rest of the lime in a bag for serving later in the week), and a pinch of salt.

3 Spread 1 tablespoon of the citrus butter on top of each fillet of fish. Cover the baking dish with plastic wrap and store overnight in the fridge; you'll be cooking this fresh prior to serving.

4 Store the remaining 4 tablespoons butter, covered, in the fridge to serve with the corn later in the week. Store the lemon rounds in a small resealable bag in the fridge until ready to cook the fish.

HOT TIP

- If you're making this as a stand-alone recipe, head to page 223 for cooking directions.

8 Honey Mustard Sauce

MAKES ABOUT 1 CUP

½ cup plus 2 tablespoons mayonnaise

2 tablespoons Dijon mustard

2 tablespoons honey

1 tablespoon rice vinegar

Kosher salt and pepper

Mix all the ingredients together in a storage jar, cover, and store in the fridge.

RALLY

Get ready to Rally! Time to take all those Prep staples and use them to create delicious meals for the week.

Citrus Butter Bass *with* Quinoa *and* Street Corn

SERVES 4

1 Preheat the oven to 400°F.

2 Remove the fish from the fridge and uncover. Scatter the lemon slices over the tops of the fillets. Bake on the top rack for 25 to 30 minutes, until the flesh flakes easily with a fork.

3 Heat the quinoa, covered, in an oven-safe baking dish in the same oven for about 15 minutes, until warm.

4 Meanwhile, line a standard baking sheet with aluminum foil. Place the corn on the baking sheet and spread all of the citrus butter to coat each one. Heat the corn in the same oven as the fish and quinoa in the final 10 minutes of their cook time. Remove the fish and quinoa from the oven (they should be hot and ready to serve now) and turn the broiler to high. Broil the corn on the top rack for 5 to 6 minutes, until charred in spots, turning every few minutes to broil all the sides. Be sure to keep an eye on the oven, as it can burn fast! Feel free to broil the fish for a minute as well, if desired.

5 Serve the fish with the quinoa and corn, topped with fresh lime juice, cilantro, and Parmesan, if desired, to make it like street corn!

RALLY INGREDIENTS

Citrus Butter Bass (page 220)

Lemon slices

Quinoa (page 216)

Corn (page 217)

4 tablespoons Citrus Butter (page 220)

Reserved lime (the one you zested), quartered

ADDITIONAL INGREDIENTS

Fresh cilantro, coarsely chopped (optional)

½ cup grated Parmesan or Cotija cheese (optional)

RALLY REMEDIES

- If you're making this vegetarian, melt the butter into roasted whole sweet potatoes and stuff with the quinoa and corn (cut the kernels from the cobs). Top with loads of cheese, lime, and cilantro!

- Turn this into fish tacos to make the meal more fun. Flake the fish and serve in soft tortillas or hard taco shells loaded with the corn, herbs, and other fixins you love!

Crispy Chicken Katsu *with* Honey Mustard Sauce *and* Asparagus

SERVES 4

RALLY INGREDIENTS

Asparagus (page 217)

Crispy Chicken Katsu in egg mixture and bag of prepared panko mixture (page 219)

½ recipe Honey Mustard Sauce (page 220)

ADDITIONAL INGREDIENTS

Neutral cooking oil or spray, for greasing

Hot sauce (optional)

1 Remove the asparagus and chicken from the fridge.

2 To bake the chicken: Preheat the oven to 425°F. Line an extra large or two standard baking sheets with parchment paper and grease the parchment liberally with oil. If you prefer to fry, skip ahead for directions.

3 Working with 2 pieces at a time, use tongs to remove the chicken from the bag of egg mixture and place into the bag of panko. Seal the bag, and shake to coat every nook and cranny. Press down on the bag to ensure crumbs have fully adhered to the chicken, and then place the coated pieces on the baking sheet. Continue with the remaining pieces, working in batches until all of the chicken is on the baking sheet(s). Drizzle or spray the tops with more oil to coat very well. Bake for about 20 minutes, until cooked through, golden, and crisp.

4 To fry the chicken: Bread the chicken using the same method as the baking directions. Coat the bottom of a large skillet with ½ inch of neutral cooking oil and heat over medium-high heat. Once hot, add the chicken to the pan, 3 or 4 pieces at a time, and fry for 4 to 5 minutes, until deeply golden brown and crisp. Flip and fry an additional 4 to 5 minutes on the second side, then transfer to a paper towel–lined plate. Repeat with the remaining chicken, wiping out the pan as needed to remove loose crumbs and adding more oil when the pan seems dry.

5 Serve the chicken katsu dunked or doused in the honey mustard sauce and with a good drizzle of hot sauce, if you want to take it to the next level. Serve with the asparagus at room temperature.

RALLY REMEDIES

- Get your kids involved with this meal. They will love shaking the chicken in the bag of bread crumbs!

- The chicken katsu is also awesome doused and served with hot honey! Buy some ready-made or mix together equal parts honey and Cholula or Frank's RedHot hot sauce.

- Serve chicken katsu sandwiches to make it a handheld meal.

- If you're making this vegetarian, bake or fry the eggplant using the same general directions as the chicken (or see page 219).

Chicken Meatloaf Sandwiches

SERVES 4

Preheat the oven to 300°F. Warm the meatloaf, covered, in an oven-safe storage container or dish for 25 minutes, or until warm. Toast buns in the same oven. Serve the sliced meatloaf in sandwiches, loaded with honey mustard sauce, sliced tomato, some lettuce, and pickles on the side. Add some basil for an additional pop of flavor, if desired.

RALLY INGREDIENTS

Meatloaf (page 218)

½ recipe Honey Mustard (page 220)

ADDITIONAL INGREDIENTS

4 to 6 ciabatta or burger buns

1 ripe large tomato, thinly sliced

1 head Bibb lettuce, washed and leaves separated

Pickles to serve

Fresh basil (optional)

RALLY REMEDIES

• You can also serve this as a plated salad topped with slices of meatloaf.

• Leftover meatloaf makes the greatest filling for a panini, and it also freezes beautifully!

Balsamic Onion Sheet Pan Pizza

SERVES 4

RALLY INGREDIENTS

Balsamic Jammy Onions
(page 216)

ADDITIONAL INGREDIENTS

Light olive oil or cooking oil
spray, for greasing

2 pounds store-bought pizza
dough, at room temperature

Kosher salt

2½ cups shredded mozzarella
cheese

GARNISHES (Optional, But Highly Encouraged)

Zest of 1 lemon

Fresh basil leaves, roughly torn

Handful of arugula

½ cup crumbled feta or Cotija
cheese

Red chile flakes or sliced
Calabrian chiles, for topping

1 Preheat the oven to 550°F. Brush a standard baking sheet with 3 to 4 tablespoons of oil or spray with cooking oil spray.

2 Stretch out the dough as much as possible in your hands and place it in the greased baking sheet, starting to shape it into a rectangle as best as possible. Cover with plastic wrap and let rise in a warm place for 10 minutes. Uncover, continue to press out the dough to the edges of the pan, and cover once more; let rise for 10 minutes. Stretch it once more, pushing the dough up the edges of the pan to make a crust. The dough should be completely relaxed by now and able to stretch out fully to the size of the pan. If the dough is a little sticky, just add some flour.

3 Season the dough with a sprinkle of salt (my secret to flavorful pizza!) and top with the mozzarella and then the jammy onions.

4 Bake on the bottom rack for about 25 minutes, until deeply golden and cooked through. Top with your garnishes of choice, cut into squares, and serve.

RALLY REMEDIES

- I like to prep my dough in the baking sheet in the morning on the day I plan to serve the pizza and let it sit at room temperature all day until dinner. The longer it sits, the better! But if you're in a rush (or your dough is frozen), you can place it in a plastic bag and seal tightly, then submerge the bag in a bowl of warm water for 20 minutes to let the dough warm and become more workable.

- Feeling extra lazy or short on time? I totally get it. Make grilled cheese or quesadillas with the balsamic onions and arugula and serve it with a glass of wine for an insanely delicious and sophisticated yet simple meal. If you have any leftover corn from the week, be sure to cut it off the cob and throw it on there as well!

PART 3

Extra Goodies

Recipes to Round Out Your Week and Use Up What's Left!

Leftovers have a bad rap. It's such a shame, because they really can save so much time and money. If you've been reading up to this page, you may have noticed that I like to intentionally plan for leftovers, which I then repurpose and turn into new meals later in the week. It's the Prep + Rally way! Sometimes "leftovers" just need a squeeze of fresh lemon juice or some chopped fresh herbs to wake them up again. Other times, they need to be introduced to new ingredients to give them new life. There is almost always a way. For everything else, there's eggs. Even *I* don't always have time to prep ahead, and eggs save me on those busy days.

When it comes to sweets and snacks, we keep things simple, fun, and somewhat healthy. I love to make prep-ahead breakfasts for those run-out-the-door mornings, and all the better if I can use up what I already have at home. I love sharing base recipes and then giving you all the options to make it your own because nobody wants to (or ever should) make a special trip to the grocery store for that one ingredient they're missing. Let's just say you're going to love these recipes.

CHAPTER 11

Leftovers Remix

My goal is to show you how to creatively inject new life into leftovers in order to keep them out of the garbage can. Not only will you be saving money, you might even fall in love with the challenge of reinventing leftovers, as I have. These recipes are meant to inspire and light that creative fuel inside you! Bookmark this page and come back to it any time you need some inspiration.

The Leftovers Guide

Chicken

Chicken salad sandwiches (page 259), chicken potpie, egg rolls (page 43), chicken pizza, chicken pasta, tacos, chicken flautas, stir-fry, pulled BBQ chicken sliders or tacos, chicken and rice bake (page 244), chicken salad (page 256)

Salmon and other flaky fish

Fish burgers, salmon salad (to replace tuna), lemony salmon pasta (page 255), fish flautas (page 181, made with fish), fish tacos, salmon fried rice, fish rillettes, fish curry, fish chowder, summer rolls

Rice, quinoa, and other grains

Fried rice (page 268), rice pudding, arancini, fried rice cakes (page 240), rice and veggie casserole, leftover grains porridge (page 243), sushi latkes, grain bowls (page 216), stuffed peppers or zucchini, baked goods, quinoa lasagna, veggie burgers

Brisket and ground beef

Egg rolls (page 43, using barbacoa from page 194), nachos, tacos. brisket chili (page 95, adding leftover brisket), enchiladas, hash, flautas, burritos, moussaka, beef-stuffed peppers, tacos, leftover meaty spaghetti (page 247), sweet potato loaded sloppy Joes, beef larb in lettuce cups, poutine

Roasted vegetables

Quiche, veggie frittata (page 265), vegetable lasagna, pizza toppers, vegetable soup, vegetable egg rolls, quesadillas, tomato and veggie ragù, veggie and sausage hash, calzones, pasta, pizza, stir-fry, grilled veggie kebabs, galette (page 252)

Overripe produce

Cobbler, jam, smoothie (page 276), fridge cleanout pie (page 291), salsa (pages 177 and 198), soup, stir-fry, ice pops

Herbs

Pesto (page 271), dressing, freezer herb-oil cubes, homemade herbed compound butter, chimichurri (page 140), infused oil, marinade, dressing

Bread

Strata (page 248), bread crumbs, bread pudding, french toast, croutons, stuffing, panzanella salad, binder for meatballs

ESSENTIAL REPURPOSING METHODS

**Throw it
in a taco shell**

**Serve it
on a bun**

**Cook it in
a casserole**

**Stir in
an egg**

**Roll it into
an egg roll**

**Cook it in a
waffle maker**

**Load it into
a sandwich**

**Blend it
into a soup**

**Puree it into a
sauce or pesto**

**Wrap it
in a burrito**

**Bake it
in a pie**

**Freeze for
a smoothie**

**Fold up a
quesadilla**

**Mix up
a stir-fry**

**Load up
a grain bowl**

**Broil up
a pizza**

**Chop up
a salad**

**Fry up
fritters**

**Stuff some
vegetables**

**Simmer some
porridge**

Fried Rice Cakes

MAKES 10 RICE CAKES AND ¾ CUP CREMA

FOR THE RICE CAKES

2 cups cooked rice or any other leftover grain

2 large eggs

3 tablespoons all-purpose or whole-wheat flour

½ teaspoon kosher salt

½ teaspoon garlic powder

¼ teaspoon pepper

¾ cup shredded mozzarella cheese

½ cup chopped fresh herbs or finely chopped roasted vegetables (optional)

Neutral oil, for frying

FOR THE LEMON CREMA

½ cup sour cream or Greek yogurt

Zest and juice of 1 lemon (3 tablespoons juice)

¼ teaspoon kosher salt

⅛ teaspoon pepper

½ teaspoon white truffle oil (optional)

This recipe is great for repurposing just about any leftover cooked grain you have on hand. It also makes for a much cleaner dinner, as it avoids the "sticky rice all over the floor" situation. Switch it up by throwing in some leftover roasted vegetables from the week. I love adding broccoli, Brussels sprouts, mushrooms, zucchini, and peas. See my hot tips for some different ways you can serve these. They're always a winner!

1 Make the rice cakes: In a medium bowl, stir together the rice, eggs, flour, salt, garlic powder, pepper, mozzarella, and herbs until combined. In a large nonstick skillet, heat 1 to 2 tablespoons oil over high heat. Working in batches, scoop ¼-cup portions of the rice mixture into the pan. Flatten with a spatula and fry until golden on both sides, 3 to 4 minutes per side. Transfer to a plate and repeat with the remaining rice mixture.

2 Make the crema: In a small bowl, whisk together all the crema ingredients.

3 Serve the hot rice cakes loaded with the crema!

HOT TIPS

- Cut this recipe in half or double it to use up any leftover grains you have on hand!

- I love frying these up and serving with toasted nori and lightly seared salmon or spicy tuna for a quick dinner. Turn them into pizzas by serving with marinara sauce for dunking. Salsa, guacamole, and sour cream turn these into a fun fiesta. How about a quick breakfast topped with a poached egg, lox, and chives? They're delicious any way you fry 'em, so think of this recipe as your little black dress and then go wild with your styling!

- Feel free to throw some finely diced cucumber (and even mint) into the crema to make more of a tzatziki sauce. Serve with some salmon, and you have the ultimate meal.

Go-To Leftover Grains Porridge

SERVES 3 OR 4

There's nothing more comforting than a big bowl of creamy porridge. I love using up any and all leftover grains from the week to make this quick and delicious breakfast. Make things more fun by prepping a batch and displaying all the topping options on the table (I love using a lazy Susan for this) so everyone can build their own at the breakfast table.

1 Place grains, milk, honey, cinnamon, and salt together in a small saucepan and bring to a boil over high heat. Immediately reduce the heat to maintain a simmer and cook, stirring occasionally, for about 15 minutes, until the mixture is creamy. Make sure the heat isn't too high or the porridge will boil over!

2 Mix in the butter and cook for 3 to 4 minutes more. Pour into bowls and top with fruit or nuts, then serve.

2 cups leftover cooked grains (rice, quinoa, farro, wheat berries, etc., or a blend)

2 cups milk of choice, plus more as needed

¼ cup honey

Pinch of ground cinnamon

Pinch of kosher salt

1 tablespoon unsalted butter

Fruit or nuts, for topping

HOT TIP

• The mixture will thicken as it cools. Just add more milk if you want to thin it out.

One-Pot Meaty Spaghetti

SERVES 4

My kids love meat sauce. They always ask me to to sign them up for hot lunch at school just so they can take part in spaghetti-and-meat-sauce day. I made a version that not only repurposes leftover meat but cooks all in one pot. Let's just say the kids don't ask me for hot lunch as often anymore—they love this more than the school's version!

In a large stockpot, combine the beef, marinara, stock, salt, and spaghetti and bring to a boil, uncovered, over high heat, being sure the spaghetti is submerged in the liquid. Reduce the heat to a very low boil (ensuring there is still cooking action happening and small bubbles are rising to the top), cover, and cook for 18 to 20 minutes, stirring halfway through, until the liquid has been absorbed and the pasta is al dente. Season with additional salt as needed and finish with a few tablespoons of good quality extra-virgin olive oil. Garnish with basil and chile flakes, if desired, and serve.

1 to 1½ cups leftover seasoned and browned ground beef (such as from leftovers from taco night, otherwise see directions in the Hot Tips)

3 cups store-bought marinara or pasta sauce (I love Don Pepino brand)

5 cups vegetable stock

Pinch of kosher salt, plus more as needed

16 ounces white spaghetti, cracked in half

Good-quality extra-virgin olive oil for finishing

Fresh basil and red chile flakes, to finish (optional)

HOT TIPS

- To use raw ground beef instead of leftover cooked beef, heat 2 tablespoons light olive oil in the stockpot over high heat. Add 1 to 1½ pounds ground beef, season with a pinch each of salt, some garlic powder, and onion powder, and cook, stirring and breaking up the meat as it cooks, until browned. Continue with the recipe as directed.

- Make this vegetarian by using Beyond Beef, or omit the meat altogether and in its place sauté some finely diced vegetables such as carrots, parsnips, celery, and mushrooms (or use up leftover veggies you have on hand) to make it more of a one-pot veggie pasta. Just be sure to sauté the vegetables first until tender and then continue as directed.

Everything Bagel Strata

SERVES 6 TO 8

12 large eggs

1½ cups whole milk

¾ teaspoon kosher salt

¼ teaspoon pepper

½ teaspoon garlic powder

Light olive oil or cooking oil spray, for greasing

5 everything bagels, preferably 1 to 2 days old, torn or cut into 1-inch pieces

2 cups shredded mozzarella cheese

½ cup thinly sliced scallions, divided

3 tablespoons unsalted butter, cut into small cubes and chilled

4 to 6 ounces lox, roughly torn, for serving

8 ounces feta, for serving (optional)

If you're looking for your next go-to brunch recipe, look no further. We're using up old bagels in these delicious stratas, but of course you can use fresh bread or any other bread you have on hand that you're looking to get rid of. I've included savory and sweet versions because I just couldn't decide which was better. Why choose when you can have both?

1 In a large bowl, whisk together the eggs, milk, salt, pepper, and garlic powder.

2 Grease a 9 x 13-inch baking dish with oil. Place the bagel pieces in the baking dish. Add the cheese and ¼ cup of the scallions, then pour the egg mixture over top. Mix until all the bagels are coated and somewhat submerged in the egg mixture. Distribute the butter pieces all over the top. Let sit on the counter for 10 minutes so the bread continues to soak up the egg. (For an even easier breakfast, prep this the night before and let it sit, covered, in the fridge until ready to bake in the morning.)

3 When ready to cook, preheat the oven to 375°F.

4 Bake, uncovered, for 35 to 40 minutes, until the top is golden. Top with the remaining ¼ cup scallions, the lox, and feta (if using) and serve immediately.

HOT TIPS

- You can make this with any savory bagel and simply add 3 tablespoons everything bagel seasoning (found in most grocery stores in the spice section) to give it the same flavor.

- This can be made with any leftover bread, but I prefer heartier breads like bagels and baguettes because they retain some texture and bite; sandwich bread becomes more of a bread pudding.

Cinnamon Sugar Bagel Strata

SERVES 6 TO 8

Like french toast's prettier and smarter sister, this dish is straight-up finger-lickin' good. The layer of sticky caramel on the bottom is glorious and something my kids fight over. I especially love that you can prep this in advance and bake it fresh in the morning. Don't we all love a good prep-ahead dish? Heck, by now you know I do!

Cooking oil spray

8 large eggs

1½ cups whole milk

½ cup pure maple syrup

1 teaspoon ground cinnamon, divided

1 teaspoon vanilla extract

Big pinch of kosher salt, plus more if needed

Pinch of ground nutmeg

5 plain bagels, torn or cut into 1-inch pieces

½ cup (1 stick) unsalted butter

½ cup dark brown sugar

2 tablespoons granulated sugar, for topping

1 Preheat the oven to 375°F. Lightly grease a 9 x 13-inch baking dish with cooking oil spray.

2 In a large bowl, whisk together the eggs, milk, maple syrup, ½ teaspoon of the cinnamon, the vanilla, salt, and nutmeg. Once combined, add the bagel pieces and stir to coat in the egg mixture. Let sit for about 15 minutes to soak up the egg mixture, or store in the fridge overnight.

3 While the bagels are soaking, in a small saucepan, melt the stick of butter over medium-low heat. Once melted, add the brown sugar, and a big pinch of salt. Raise the heat to medium and whisk until the mixture is thoroughly combined and caramel-like, about 5 minutes. Carefully pour the mixture into the greased baking dish and spread it evenly over the bottom.

4 Add the bagel mixture to the baking dish with the caramel mixture. Sprinkle the top of the strata with the remaining ½ teaspoon cinnamon and the granulated sugar and bake for 35 to 40 minutes, until the top is golden brown. Serve piping hot.

HOT TIPS

- Add chocolate chips to switch it up!

- Make these in individual ramekins. Simply decrease the bake time a tad and cook until tops are golden.

Cheesy Spinach Galette

MAKES 2 GALETTES

1 (16-ounce) bag frozen spinach, thawed and squeezed/drained very well (or use 2 to 3 cups leftover roasted vegetables of your choice)

1 cup ricotta cheese (cottage cheese works too!)

2 cups shredded mozzarella cheese

1 large egg

½ onion, finely diced

¾ teaspoon kosher salt

½ teaspoon garlic powder

½ teaspoon onion powder

¼ teaspoon pepper

2 (9-inch) store-bought pie crusts, thawed

1 large egg yolk, mixed with a splash of water, for egg wash

1 Preheat the oven to 350°F and set aside 2 standard baking sheets.

2 In a large bowl, mix the spinach, ricotta, mozzarella, egg, onion, salt, garlic powder, onion powder, and pepper until combined.

3 Place a sheet of parchment paper (large enough to fit a standard baking sheet) on the counter and roll out one of the pie crusts on the parchment. Lift up the parchment with the rolled-out dough and place it on one of the baking sheets. Repeat with the second pie crust so that you have two baking sheets, each with one rolled-out sheet of dough. Fill the center of each pie crust with half the spinach mixture, leaving a 1- to 2-inch border for the crust. Gently fold the border of the pie crust over the filling, leaving the filling at the center exposed.

4 Brush the egg wash over the crusts. Bake on the middle and bottom racks for 35 to 45 minutes, until the crust is golden brown and glossy, swapping the pans halfway through so each has equal time on the middle rack. Let cool for about 5 minutes before slicing into wedges and serving.

I started making galettes when I was cooking for a client in the Hamptons in New York years ago. I made individual farm-fresh blueberry galettes and served them with ice cream, and boy, did they go over well. Since then, I've been making savory galettes as a way to repurpose leftover veggies from the week. This recipe uses frozen spinach, but you can swap the spinach out for 2 to 3 cups of leftover roasted vegetables from the week such as broccoli, cauliflower, zucchini, etc. It's such a fabulous way to repurpose those leftovers and give them new life. Have some fun with this recipe and make it your own.

HOT TIP

- I love using a salad spinner or nut-milk bag for wringing out the spinach. These can be found very inexpensively online or in most home goods stores and are super-useful tools to have in your kitchen.

Lemony Salmon Pasta

SERVES 4

Leftover fish is tricky because leftovers don't keep long in the fridge and fish isn't too appealing when reheated. Sometimes I turn the leftovers into a salmon salad loaded with dill, pickles, and mayo, similar to tuna salad, to eat with crackers or in a sandwich. Other times I opt to make a salmon pasta, because both kids and adults love it and it's a sure way to make your leftover fish shine again! The tahini gives the pasta such richness and depth of flavor and contributes to the creamy texture, while the lemon makes it all pop.

1 Bring a large pot of water to a boil. Cook the pasta according to the package directions until al dente. Drain, without rinsing, and set aside.

2 Meanwhile, in a large skillet, heat the olive oil over medium heat. Add the garlic and cook until fragrant, being careful not to burn it. Add the flour and whisk for a few seconds to mix it into the oil. Add the milk, tahini, salt, and pepper. Reduce the heat to maintain a simmer and cook for 3 to 4 minutes, until the sauce is thick enough to coat the back of a spoon. Add the pasta, salmon, peas, and lemon zest and juice and mix to combine and coat with the sauce, then cook for 1 minute more. Remove from the heat. Mix in the Parmesan and season with additional salt and pepper as needed, then serve.

16 ounces white bow-tie pasta

3 tablespoons light olive oil

5 garlic cloves, minced

2 tablespoons all-purpose flour

3 cups whole milk

1 tablespoon tahini

1¼ teaspoons kosher salt, plus more if needed

¼ teaspoon pepper, plus more if needed

1½ cups flaked leftover cooked salmon (in bite-size pieces)

1½ cups frozen peas, thawed

Zest and juice of 1 lemon (3 tablespoons juice)

⅓ cup grated Parmesan cheese

HOT TIPS

• You can make this recipe with any fish you love or have on hand or keep it vegetarian by omitting the fish altogether. It's a great stand-alone lemony pasta.

• If you don't have leftover salmon and want to cook some fresh, simply roast a 1-pound piece of boneless, skinless salmon. Drizzle with oil and season with salt and pepper or even some Old Bay seasoning for quick flavor. Roast at 400°F until easily flaked with a fork, 12 to 15 minutes.

California Chicken Salad

SERVES 4 (MAKES 1 CUP DRESSING)

All the flavors I love, laced with some California vibes. This salad is so fresh and it's a major crowd-pleaser, not to mention a great way to use up last night's roast chicken! Mix up the salad by adding napa cabbage, crunchy tortilla chips, cucumber, etc. You're going to love this one.

FOR THE SALAD

4 cups finely shredded purple cabbage (10 ounces)

1 red bell pepper, thinly sliced

3 scallions, thinly sliced

1 ripe yet firm medium mango, peeled and diced

1 large avocado, diced

5 radishes, thinly sliced

½ cup roasted salted cashews, coarsely chopped

2 cooked chicken breasts, diced (1½ cups), at room temperature

FOR THE SESAME-LIME DRESSING

Zest and juice of 3 limes (6 tablespoons juice)

¼ cup white wine vinegar

1 teaspoon toasted sesame oil

1 tablespoon natural cashew or peanut butter

3 tablespoons fresh parsley or cilantro, roughly torn, plus more for garnish

2 tablespoons pure maple syrup

1 garlic clove, peeled

½ to 1 small jalapeño, seeded and coarsely chopped (optional)

¼ cup extra-virgin olive oil

Kosher salt and pepper

1 Make the salad: Combine all the salad ingredients in a large bowl. Set aside while you make the dressing.

2 Make the dressing: Combine all the dressing ingredients in a wide-mouthed jar and blend with an immersion blender until smooth. Taste for seasoning and add more salt and pepper as needed.

3 Pour the dressing over the salad and toss to coat. Serve immediately.

Grilled Chicken Pita Pockets

SERVES 4

I'm going to let you in on a little secret. There are two dishes I've always loathed: cold pasta salads and cold chicken salads. I've decided to give chicken salad an upgrade (sorry, mister cold pasta salad, but I don't think I'll ever find a way to love you!). You're going to love this grilled pita sandwich. It's the most flavor-packed pita pocket you'll ever have, and it gets grilled to perfection—as warm is the only way to go, in my opinion.

1 In a large bowl, whisk together the sun-dried tomatoes and oil, lemon zest and juice, capers and brine, garlic powder, mayonnaise, basil, and pinches of salt and pepper. Stir in the chicken.

2 Heat a grill pan, panini press, or heavy-bottomed pan on medium heat and grease with some oil. Stuff the chicken salad and some arugula into the pita pockets and grill for about 2 minutes per side to warm through, then serve.

¼ cup sun-dried tomatoes packed in oil, drained and minced, plus 3 tablespoons oil from the jar

Zest and juice of 1 lemon (3 tablespoons juice)

1 tablespoon capers, minced, plus 2 teaspoons brine from the jar

¼ teaspoon garlic powder

3 tablespoons mayonnaise

2 tablespoons fresh basil or tarragon leaves, finely chopped

Kosher salt and pepper

3 cooked chicken breasts, shredded (about 3 cups)

Oil for greasing

2 pitas, halved

Handful of arugula

HOT TIPS

- I save the oil from the sun-dried tomatoes and use it as a quick flavor booster. Make a batch of fresh pasta and toss it in some sun-dried tomato oil, fresh lemon zest and juice, and lots of grated Parmesan. It's delicious and elegant, yet approachable for the whole family.

- Make this chicken salad into a salmon salad! I also love using flaky white fish in place of the chicken.

- Switch up the flavors to make over this chicken salad multiple ways. Try curry, apples, raisins, and tarragon. Or olives, diced red pepper, and parsley. How about dill, pepperoncini, scallion, and canned marinated artichokes. The combinations are endless!

CHAPTER 12

Last-Minute Scramble

There are days even *I* don't feel like cooking, let alone meal prepping on a busy Sunday! My fall-back plan for a quick weeknight dinner? EGGS! They're like a best friend you can always rely on. They're always waiting for you in the fridge. They make a complete meal. They please all. And they are so incredibly versatile. Crack this s-egg-tion open and get scramblin'.

Chilaquiles

SERVES 2

2 to 3 tablespoons light olive oil, for frying

2 large eggs

2 cups Salsa Roja (page 177)

4 handfuls of tortilla chips

½ avocado, cubed

1 handful cilantro, coarsely chopped

¼ cup crumbled feta or Cotija cheese

My love affair with chilaquiles became obvious when I ordered them every single morning on a recent trip to Mexico. I would order the dish "Christmas style" as they called it; half verde and half roja because I couldn't decide which I loved more. I love making a double batch of salsa at the start of the week to enhance dinner and also allow for delicious breakfasts all week long that bring me right back to Mexico.

1 In a nonstick skillet, heat the oil over high heat. Fry 2 eggs until golden and crisp, 3 to 4 minutes, until the whites are set. Feel free to flip and cook the other side if you prefer, or leave the eggs sunny side up. Slide the eggs onto a plate while you prepare the rest.

2 Heat the salsa in the pan for 2 to 3 minutes until it starts to bubble and add the chips. Toss to coat together and cook for a minute or two until the chips start to soften ever so slightly.

3 Serve on plates, topped with the fried eggs and avocado. Garnish with the cilantro and feta for an extra pop of flavor.

HOT TIPS

• You can also make this with Salsa Verde (page 198) or with your favorite store-bought salsa!

• For another way to enjoy salsa for breakfast, try scrambling an egg, stuffing it inside a freshly charred soft corn tortilla, adding slices of avocado, and dousing it with lots of salsa and hot sauce.

Veggie Frittata

SERVES 4

You can't beat a frittata. Not only does it get more veggies into your diet, but it's the best way to repurpose leftover roasted vegetables from the week or to use up vegetables and herbs you're looking to clean out of the fridge. Use this recipe as a jumping-off point and throw in whatever you have on hand. The sky's the limit when it comes to flavor combos, but here are some of my favorites:

- *Roasted mushrooms, broccoli, and basil*
- *Sautéed onions, peppers, jalapeño, and cilantro*
- *Sautéed spinach or kale, garlic, and dill*
- *Roasted potatoes, peas, and thyme*

1 Preheat the oven to 400°F.

2 In a large nonstick oven-safe skillet, heat the oil over high heat. Add the onion, pepper, and mushrooms and sauté for 8 minutes, or until softened and most of the moisture from the mushrooms has evaporated.

3 Meanwhile, in a medium bowl, whisk together the eggs, cottage cheese, mozzarella, salt, paprika, and pepper. Pour the mixture into the hot pan and stir to distribute the vegetables evenly. Cook for a minute or so, then carefully transfer to the oven and bake for 20 minutes, or until set. Let cool slightly and then cut into wedges. Serve with hot sauce and feta.

1 to 2 tablespoons light olive oil

1 onion, finely diced

1 red bell pepper, finely diced

8 ounces mushrooms, finely diced

8 large eggs

¾ cup cottage cheese (I prefer whipped cottage cheese)

½ cup shredded mozzarella cheese

¾ teaspoon kosher salt

½ teaspoon paprika

¼ teaspoon pepper

Hot sauce, for serving

Crumbled feta or Cotija cheese, for serving

HOT TIPS

- Use this mixture to make individual muffin cups (use silicone baking cups to ensure they come out of the pan), or even as a scramble for a faster meal.

- To use up leftover roasted vegetables from the week, swap out the onion, peppers, and mushrooms for 1 to 2 cups chopped roasted vegetables. Mix together in a bowl with the eggs, cheeses, and spices and continue as directed.

Salmon *and* Rice Bowls *with* 7-Minute Eggs

SERVES 4

4 center-cut salmon fillets, 4 to 5 ounces each

Kosher salt and pepper

1 tablespoon light olive oil

4 large eggs

Sushi Rice (page 94), with or without the maple-vinegar seasoning

2 avocados, sliced

Soy sauce (or Poke Marinade, page 98)

Optional toppings: toasted nori, hot sauce, mayonnaise, sesame seeds, cucumbers, shredded carrots, scallions, and fresh cilantro

This is the simplest meal that wins every time, and I take pride in the fact that I've been making it well before it became trendy on TikTok! I love it for lunch or dinner, and when I already have most of the components prepped from the week, it's a cinch to throw together. You can jazz it up a million different ways. Throw a different sauce on it, add some pickled veggies, or even swap out the salmon for tofu. This is your dish. Build it any way your heart desires.

---

1 Preheat the broiler to high with the rack set to the highest position. Line a standard baking sheet with aluminum foil.

2 Place the salmon on the baking sheet. Season with salt and pepper and coat with the oil. Broil for 5 to 7 minutes, until easily flaked with a fork.

3 Meanwhile, fill a small saucepan halfway with water and add a big pinch of salt. Bring to a boil. Carefully lower in the eggs and boil for exactly 7 minutes, if you like your egg jammy yet slightly runny. (Go for 9 minutes if you like it fully hard-boiled but still creamy.) Meanwhile fill a medium bowl halfway with water and some ice. Set aside. Remove the eggs from the saucepan and plunge them into the ice water. Let the eggs cool for 3 to 4 minutes before peeling.

4 To serve, divide the rice among four bowls and top with the salmon, avocado, egg, and soy sauce. Garnish with toasted nori or any other toppings of choice.

HOT TIPS

- You can also roll these into nori hand rolls or let everyone DIY! I like to make a spicy mayo (mix mayo and sriracha, or go for mayo and ketchup for the kids) to spread over the base of the nori and then add rice, flaked salmon, chopped-up egg, and avocado. Roll up like a burrito or into cones and serve with soy sauce or poke marinade.

Salami *and* Egg Fried Rice

SERVES 4

3 tablespoons light olive oil, divided

2 cups bite-size pieces soft salami (about half of a salami)

3 cups leftover cooked rice (or about 1½ cups uncooked, prepared according to the package directions)

1 cup frozen peas and carrots

¼ cup thinly sliced scallions

5 tablespoons low-sodium soy sauce

4 large eggs

Kosher salt and pepper

Growing up, my sisters and I ate a lot of salami and eggs. It was always our go-to late-night snack. This dish is super nostalgic, but I've mashed it up with fried rice—why not marry two crave-worthy dishes?

In a large skillet, heat 1 tablespoon of the oil over high heat. Add the salami and fry until crisp and golden. Add another tablespoon of the oil, then add the rice, peas and carrots, scallions, and soy sauce and cook, stirring, for 4 to 5 minutes, until the mixture is warmed through and the vegetables have thawed. Push the rice to the side and add the remaining 1 tablespoon of oil to the exposed pan. Crack the eggs into the pan and scramble with a fork, then mix the scrambled eggs into the rice mixture. Season to taste and serve.

HOT TIP

• If you have a little extra time on your hands (said no parent ever!), throw in some minced ginger and garlic right after the salami is fried for an additional boost of flavor.

Easy Cheesy Eggies *in* Stars

SERVES 2 (MAKES 4 SLICES)

The classic egg-in-a-frame just got a little makeover! The addition of tuna makes this dish a meal and gives it a whole new flavor profile. My girls love a good ol' breakfast-for-dinner situation and are always first in line to help make it happen.

1 In a medium bowl, whisk together the eggs, salt, pepper, and paprika. Add the mozzarella and tuna and mix together.

2 Using a cookie cutter (we love the star shape!) or the rim of a small cup small enough to fit within the crust of the bread, punch out a hole in the center of each slice of bread. Save the cut-out centers for toasting.

3 In a large skillet, heat 1 to 2 tablespoons of the oil over medium-high heat. Add 2 slices of bread plus the cut-out centers in a single layer in the pan. Immediately pour one-quarter of the egg mixture into the hole in each slice of bread and cook for 2 to 3 minutes, until set on the bottom. Flip (flipping the cutouts as well) and cook for a minute or two on the second side. Transfer everything to a plate. Add the remaining oil to the pan and repeat with the remaining bread and egg mixture.

4 Serve on plates, garnished with additional paprika, with the toasted cutouts alongside.

2 large eggs

¼ teaspoon kosher salt

⅛ teaspoon pepper

½ teaspoon smoked paprika, plus more for garnish

¼ cup shredded mozzarella cheese

2 tablespoons drained canned tuna (half a 5-ounce can)

2 to 3 tablespoons light oil or cooking oil spray, for greasing

4 slices sandwich bread

HOT TIP

- The addition of tuna gives this dish tuna melt vibes, but if you're not the biggest tuna fan, feel free to omit. Use chopped smoked salmon or smoked white fish. It's delicious either way, and everyone's happy because you can customize each one.

Pesto *and* Egg Flowers

SERVES 4 (MAKES 1 CUP PESTO)

This is the kind of last-minute meal that gets more awesome when you have some prepped pesto already waiting for you in the fridge from the week. Slather it on some bread with the toppings and enjoy a meal in minutes. Feel free to use up leftover Broccoli Pesto (page 52) or even Salsa Verde (page 198) for a totally different flavor. As always, there are no rules, and eggs just always seem to work any which way.

1 Preheat the oven to 425°F. Line a standard baking sheet with parchment paper.

2 Make the pesto: In a food processor, combine the basil, garlic, pine nuts, and Parmesan. Process to combine, then, with the motor running, slowly add the oil and process until smooth. Add extra oil as needed if it seems too thick and season with salt and pepper to taste.

3 Place the flatbreads on the prepared baking sheet. Spread some pesto on each flatbread and top with 2 pepper rings. Bake for 5 minutes in the center rack. Pull out the baking sheet halfway and crack 2 eggs onto each flatbread in the center of the pepper rings. Bake for 8 to 10 minutes more, until the eggs are cooked to your desired doneness. Serve hot, with more shaved Parmesan.

FOR THE PESTO

4 cups fresh basil leaves

2 garlic cloves, peeled

½ cup pine nuts or walnuts

1 cup grated Parmesan cheese

¼ cup extra-virgin olive oil, plus more as needed

Kosher salt and pepper

TO ASSEMBLE

4 flatbreads or naan

2 medium red bell peppers, thinly sliced horizontally into 8 rings

8 large eggs

Shaved Parmesan cheese

HOT TIP

• Switch things up and make pita pizzas instead. Place pitas on a parchment-lined baking sheet and slather the tops with pesto. Top with cheese, olives, artichokes, and any other toppings you love. Bake for 10 to 15 minutes at 425°F until crisp and then cut into triangles.

CHAPTER 13

Sweets, Snacks, *and* Everything *in* Between

I'm not much of a baker, as I've always found it to be too restricting. Since baking is more of a science, if you mess up one little measurement, the cake flops, turns green (yes, this has happened to me before with sunflower butter!), or tastes rancid. Because of that, I like to stick to simple baking recipes that are forgiving yet delicious and can be tweaked slightly to make them your own. I love to bake on the healthier side when possible. I'm always a fan of a good multipurpose recipe, and I'm forever trying to concoct new prep-ahead recipes. That's basically what you'll find in this chapter. These are the family favorites that we make week after week. Dive on in!

Crazy Kitchen Sink Cookies

MAKES 18 COOKIES

1¾ cups all-purpose flour

¾ teaspoon baking powder

½ teaspoon baking soda

¼ teaspoon kosher salt

½ cup (1 stick) unsalted butter

¾ cup dark brown sugar

½ cup granulated sugar

1 large egg

1 large egg yolk

1 teaspoon vanilla extract

2 tablespoons tahini paste

3 tablespoons white or yellow light miso

1 tablespoon low-sodium soy sauce

1 tablespoon toasted sunflower seeds

½ cup potato chips

1 cup crushed pretzels

¾ cup semisweet chocolate chips

1 Preheat the oven to 350°F. Line two standard baking sheets with parchment paper and position two oven racks as close to the center of the oven as possible.

2 In a large bowl, mix together the flour, baking powder, baking soda, and salt. Set aside.

3 In the bowl of a stand mixer fitted with the paddle attachment, cream the butter with the sugars until smooth. Add the egg, egg yolk, and vanilla and beat until combined. Add the tahini, miso, and soy sauce and beat for an additional minute.

4 Add the dry ingredients and mix until just incorporated. Add the sunflower seeds, potato chips, pretzels, and chocolate chips and mix on low speed for a few seconds, until fully integrated into the batter.

5 Form the dough into 18 cookies and place them on the prepared baking sheets, leaving about 3 inches between the cookies so they have room to spread. Bake the cookies for 15 to 17 minutes until the cookies are golden but still soft and the tops look cracked, swapping the pans halfway through baking. You want these to remain chewy, so don't overbake! You can also make them jumbo size and increase the bake time to 20 to 22 minutes.

6 Let cool on the pans (or a cooling rack for faster cooling) and devour!

This is the ultimate way to use up leftover bits of ingredients in your fridge and pantry. You know that chip bag that is just sitting there untouched for months with the tiniest amount left? You just found a use for it! Go wild and throw in whatever you have on hand such as M&M's, chopped nuts, and last bits of cereal. The salty/sweet/umami flavor combination is off the charts and gives these cookies a hint of toffee flavor. These are a must-make.

HOT TIP

- Make a batch of dough, roll it into a log, and freeze it wrapped up in parchment paper like a salami. When ready to use, simply cut the log into rounds, thaw on a parchment-lined baking sheet, and bake.

Anything Goes Smoothie Bowl

SERVES 3

2 cups mixed frozen fruit of choice

Handful of greens, such as fresh kale or spinach (optional)

2 very ripe large bananas, peeled and frozen

½ cup cold water or milk of choice

Big handful of ice

Add-in ideas: nut butter (I love peanut butter), flaxseeds, hemp seeds, protein powder, unsweetened cocoa powder

Topping ideas: All-Time Favorite Granola (page 285), Magic Shell, fresh berries, sliced bananas, chocolate chips, cereal

Solomon starts screaming with excitement when he sees me reaching for the blender. He and the girls are addicted to smoothies! We like our smoothies thick like ice cream because the kids feel like it's a major treat, but it's one you can feel good about serving. I love using frozen cherries and bananas because they make the texture velvety smooth. Cocoa powder always finds its way into our smoothies because it conceals any off-putting colors and makes the smoothie taste like a milkshake. Adding a scoop of your favorite protein powder and nut butter helps achieve that thick, creamy consistency that I get asked about daily on Instagram. But, as this smoothie bowl is named . . . anything goes! Use this recipe as your starting point and choose your own adventure to find out which flavor combos you like.

Place the frozen fruit, greens (if using), bananas, water, ice, and any add-ins in a high-speed blender. Blend for 30 seconds to 1 minute to make sure you achieve a thick, creamy texture. If it's too thick and won't blend, add some more water or milk a little bit at a time until you've reached the desired consistency. Pour into cups or bowls and finish with your toppings of choice, then eat with a spoon.

HOT TIPS

• Pour any leftovers into ice pop molds and freeze for later!

• I love prepping smoothie packs to save even more time throughout the week. Portion out everything besides the water or milk and ice cubes into storage bags (I love Stasher bags for this) and freeze. When you're craving a smoothie, simply pour the contents of the bag into the blender, add your water or milk and ice, and blend for a super-fast smoothie.

• You can of course omit the greens, but it's a great way to get them in!

• Cherries and mango will add more sweetness and creaminess than berries. Mix and match to find out what you enjoy.

• If you want more of a drinkable smoothie, simply add an extra ¼ to ½ cup water or milk.

Daddy Pig's Ice Cream

SERVES 2

Not sure when we started calling Mike "Daddy Pig," but it stuck, and now it's what we call him in our house. This ice cream (or thick smoothie) is special for our Daddy Pig, as he's the only one in the house who prefers more of a tart-tasting smoothie and won't eat a smoothie with bananas in it. Dates and creamy mango replace the banana's sweetness and texture and make our Daddy Pig very happy!

1 cup frozen diced mango

1 cup frozen diced pineapple

4 fat Medjool dates, pitted

½ cup milk of choice

¼ teaspoon vanilla extract

Big handful of ice

1 cup vanilla ice cream (optional)

½ cup toasted coconut flakes, for topping

Place the mango, pineapple, dates, milk, vanilla, and ice in a high-speed blender. Blend for 30 seconds to 1 minute to make sure you achieve a thick, creamy texture. If it's too thick, add some more milk, but give it a chance to blend and become thick like ice cream before adding more liquid. This can take 1 to 2 minutes to get super creamy! If you want a special treat, add the vanilla ice cream and blend for a few more seconds until mixed. Spoon into bowls or cups and top with coconut flakes.

HOT TIP

- If, like me, you love bananas in smoothies, replace the dates with 1 large banana.

Savory Spiced Popcorn

SERVES 4

Popcorn is by far the Klein family's favorite snack. When I'm lazy (always) and need a quick dessert, I'll pop some popcorn in a pot and then throw in some chocolate chips to melt right in there for a sweet and salty treat. When we're craving a more savory version, we go with this recipe. It's truly the best of all worlds, as it's the ultimate mix of sweet and salty. This popcorn hits every note and, in my opinion, is the perfect snack. You won't be running to the pantry to satisfy another craving.

¼ cup neutral oil

½ cup unpopped popcorn kernels

1¼ teaspoons kosher salt

4 tablespoons (½ stick) unsalted butter

¼ cup pure maple syrup

¼ cup nutritional yeast

1 (.17-ounce) package toasted seaweed/nori snacks, crumbled or cut into thin strips with clean scissors

1 In a 6- to 8-quart stockpot, heat the oil over high heat. Add the popcorn kernels and swirl the pot to coat them all in oil. Cover with a lid and wait until you hear popping, then reduce the heat to medium and let the kernels continue to pop, being sure that the heat remains at medium so as not to burn the popcorn. Cook for about 5 minutes or until the popping stops. Remove the lid carefully. Pour the popcorn into a large bowl and sprinkle with the salt, shaking to coat. Set aside.

2 Put the butter in the same pot you used for the popcorn and melt it over low heat. Remove from the heat (you don't want the butter mixture to be too hot when adding to the popcorn) and stir in the maple syrup—this will help cool down the butter a bit. Pour the mixture over the popcorn, mixing to coat. Add the nutritional yeast and seaweed and mix to coat the popcorn with the seasonings, then serve.

HOT TIPS

- Get the kids involved and let them have fun cutting up the nori with child-safe scissors!

- Store in an airtight container or resealable bag on the counter for up to 2 days.

- Not a fan of nutritional yeast or nori? Leave them out. Popcorn with maple butter is delicious. Add a sprinkle of cinnamon to make this more of a cinnamon roll–style popcorn, or pumpkin pie spice for all you pumpkin lovers out there. Addicting!

Chocolate Cereal Freezer Bars

SERVES 8

1 cup semi-sweet chocolate chips

1 cup mini marshmallows

½ cup unsweetened natural peanut butter

¼ cup natural tahini

½ cup pure maple syrup

4 tablespoons (½ stick) unsalted butter

6 cups randomly mixed cereal of choice (opt for low-sugar, crispy corn- or rice-based cereal for best results)

1 Fill a medium saucepan halfway with water. Place a large glass bowl over the pot and bring the water to a boil to create a double boiler. Put the chocolate chips, marshmallows, peanut butter, tahini, maple syrup, and butter in the bowl and let heat. Once the water is boiling, reduce the heat to maintain a simmer and allow the mixture to melt and come together, stirring every so often with a rubber spatula. (Alternatively, you can skip the stove and combine the ingredients in the bowl, then heat in the microwave in 30-second increments to avoid burning, stirring after each, until melted.)

2 Using a kitchen towel or oven mitt, carefully remove the hot bowl from the double boiler (the bowl will be warm and the steam from the water underneath will escape when you lift the bowl, so be careful!) and set it on the counter. Add the cereal to the bowl and mix well to coat it in the chocolate mixture.

3 Pour the mixture into a 9 x 13-inch baking dish, pressing down on it with the spatula. Wet the palm of your hand (this keeps it from sticking to you) and press down firmly, almost crushing the mixture, so it will hold together in bars. Cover with plastic wrap and freeze for at least 30 minutes before cutting into squares or rectangles. Place in bags and store in the freezer for the most addictive treat ever. Trust me on this one!

Don't you hate how bulky cereal boxes are and how kids always leave less than a bowl's worth of cereal at the bottom of the box that then goes off to get stale and take up major real estate in your pantry? End rant. Mix and match your favorites to create this chocolaty dessert and make good use of all those last bits of cereal.

HOT TIPS

- Feel free to throw in any nuts, chocolate chips, candies, or cereal varieties here! For the crispiest bars, I recommend corn- or rice-based cereals.

- Another way I like to use up cereal is to blend it in a food processor until it resembles coarse crumbs (or crush it in a resealable plastic bag) and use it as bread crumbs for chicken nuggets (try it on chicken katsu, page 219) or fish (try the Hasselback salmon on page 136). Play around with different flavor combinations and use up what you got!

Breakfast Bars

MAKES 18 BARS

4 tablespoons (½ stick) unsalted butter

½ cup pure maple syrup

3 tablespoons unsweetened natural peanut butter

1 tablespoon molasses

⅓ cup packed light brown sugar

3 cups rolled oats

⅔ cup whole-wheat flour

¾ teaspoon baking soda

½ teaspoon kosher salt

2 large egg yolks

¼ cup pine nuts, coarsely chopped

½ cup shelled unsalted pistachios, coarsely chopped

⅔ cup 70% cocoa chocolate chunks

I feel so lucky to have met some amazing women and fellow mom-preneurs over the years. My friend Erin of Totum Women created the most delicious lactation cookie mix on the market, which I became addicted to when I was nursing Solomon. We all loved them so much that I knew I needed to put my spin on them. They are, hands down, my favorite recipe in this book, and I love how they're mixed together in one pot! These cookies are perfectly chewy, not overly sweet, and you're going to fall in love with the irresistible flavor combination of the pine nuts, pistachios, and chocolate. Make a double batch . . . you've been warned!

1 Preheat the oven to 350°F. Line a standard baking sheet (or quarter sheet pan, if you have one!) with parchment paper.

2 In a 4-quart stockpot, melt the butter over high heat. Remove from the heat and mix in the maple syrup, peanut butter, molasses, and brown sugar. Add the oats, flour, baking soda, and salt and mix well to incorporate. Mix in the egg yolks. Add the pine nuts, pistachios, and chocolate chunks and stir to combine.

3 Pour the mixture out onto one side of the baking sheet. Dampen the palms of your hands with some water (to avoid sticking) and press the mixture over half the prepared baking sheet, spreading it from the center out to one of the edges. If you're using a quarter sheet pan, press the mixture into the whole pan and press down firmly.

4 Bake on the middle rack for 15 minutes. Let cool completely before cutting into bars. Make two cuts vertically so you have 3 rows, then 5 cuts horizontally so you have 18 bars. Let cool and store on the counter in an airtight bag or container.

HOT TIPS

• These freeze beautifully, so feel free to make a double batch and store in the freezer.

• Get the kids involved and let them chop the nuts: Place the nuts in a storage bag and seal the top, and then have them smash the nuts with a can or rolling pin.

• Play around with different flavor combinations, using up what you have at home. I love macadamia nuts, cranberries, and white chocolate chips.

All-Time Favorite Granola

MAKES 4 CUPS

Okay, I'm a granola snob. I really don't like any other granola but my own. This is the ultimate chewy granola that is soon to be your new favorite. I love making a big batch at the start of the week for topping smoothies and adding to Greek yogurt with honey. You can even make some granola parfaits in mason jars to take on the go. Be sure to bake the granola until it's just about to burn. That slightly burnt honey flavor is addicting!

2 cups rolled oats

½ cup hazelnuts (ideally blanched and peeled), coarsely chopped

½ cup unsweetened coconut flakes

¼ cup light olive oil

½ cup honey

⅛ teaspoon kosher salt

¼ cup dried cherries

1 Preheat the oven to 375°F. Line a standard baking sheet with parchment paper.

2 Place the oats, hazelnuts, and coconut in a mound on the prepared baking sheet. Top with the olive oil, honey, and salt and mix together with your hands until incorporated. Spread the mixture into an even layer and bake on the center rack for 16 minutes, until golden, crisp, and ever so slightly burnt—trust me!

3 Remove from the oven and add the dried cherries to the baking sheet. Mix to fully incorporate and carefully break up the granola while still hot. Let cool completely (the granola will harden as it cools), then break it all apart—get the kids involved here!—and place in an airtight container. Store on the counter for up to 1 week.

HOT TIPS

• The granola needs to be crumbled up once cooled, as the honey makes it stick together. If you want another fun way to serve this, let the granola cool, and instead of breaking it up into little granola bits, just crack it into random-sized shards. These are great to take to school and are even fun for topping with Greek yogurt, honey, and sliced fruit and eating like an open-faced sandwich!

• You can use this to top ice cream or a yogurt parfait, or to enjoy by the handful. My kids and I love making breakfast banana splits by topping sliced bananas with yogurt, granola, peanut butter, berries, and whipped cream.

Chocolate Macaroon Chia Pudding *with* Animal Crackers

SERVES 4 (MAKES 2 CUPS PUDDING)

½ cup roasted and salted cashews

2 cups water

7 Medjool dates, pitted

3 tablespoons plus 2 teaspoons unsweetened shredded coconut, divided

2 tablespoons unsweetened cocoa powder

¼ cup black chia seeds

16 animal crackers

1 In a high-speed blender, combine the cashews, water, dates, 3 tablespoons shredded coconut, and cocoa powder. Blend for 30 to 60 seconds, or until completely smooth. Add the chia seeds and blitz once or twice just to mix them in. You want them to keep their shape and texture.

2 Using four 7-ounce small storage jars, place 4 animal crackers against the sides of each jar and then pour ½ cup of the chia pudding into the center of each jar. The animal crackers should stay pressed up against the jar. Top each jar with the remaining 2 teaspoons of coconut "snow," cover, and refrigerate to thicken even more and chill. Best served cold, right out of the jar, for a quick and easy breakfast or snack!

HOT TIPS

- These are also delicious layered with berries and bananas and topped with whipped cream. Let the kids DIY their own sundaes!

- Not in the mood for chocolate? Instead of the cocoa powder and coconut, add some fresh strawberries, cinnamon, and vanilla extract. You'll end up with a delicious strawberry shortcake–style chia pudding.

- Speaking of strawberry, my neighbor Chava introduced me to the most delicious hot strawberry chia drink and I just had to re-create it. My girls and I are obsessed, and it's yet another great way to get healthy chia seeds into our diet. To make two drinks, pour 1 cup boiling water into two separate mugs. Add ¼ cup strawberry puree (simply blend thawed frozen strawberries until smooth) to each mug and add 1 tablespoon honey. Lastly, stir 1½ teaspoons chia seeds into each cup and enjoy hot! Feel free to use white chia seeds, as they tend to be more approachable for kids.

About eight years ago, I came up with three unique, superfood-packed chia pudding flavors that I hoped to sell in the yogurt section of grocery stores. It simply did not exist back then and even today it's not a common product. However, after going through rounds of food lab testing, certifications, etc., I quickly learned what an exhausting task developing a food product would be. I promised I would share it in a book someday, and here we are. This is the chocolate version, with a fun serving idea that gets kids excited about eating superfoods. It's just like chocolate pudding. Make a bunch at the start of the week to eat as a quick dessert or breakfast on the go, right out of the fridge.

Rainbow Sheet-Pancakes

SERVES 8 TO 10

FOR THE PANCAKES

1 to 2 tablespoons unsalted butter or cooking spray, for the pan

3 large eggs

2 cups milk of choice

1 cup pure maple syrup

2 cups whole-wheat flour

1 cup almond flour

2 teaspoons baking powder

1 teaspoon baking soda

1 teaspoon kosher salt

TOPPINGS

1 cup strawberries, cut into small dice

1 cup peeled small-diced fresh mango

1 cup thinly sliced bananas

1 cup thinly sliced kiwi

1 cup blueberries

Pure maple syrup

1 Preheat the oven to 500°F. Grease a standard baking sheet with the butter or cooking oil spray.

2 In a large bowl, mix together the eggs, milk, and maple syrup. Add the whole-wheat flour, almond flour, baking powder, baking soda, and salt and whisk (use an actual whisk to evenly distribute the ingredients!) until just incorporated. Pour the batter onto the prepared baking sheet. Place on the middle rack in the oven and immediately lower the oven temperature to 400°F. Bake for 15 to 18 minutes, until set and golden on top.

3 Remove from the oven and top with rows of fruit to create a rainbow. Serve hot, cut into squares, with maple syrup to top!

HOT TIPS

• Swap in any fruit your family loves or fruit that you're trying to use up! Or if your family prefers chocolate (like mine), nix the fruit altogether and mix chocolate chips into the batter before baking.

• Use all-purpose flour in place of the almond meal if you have nut allergies.

• Store leftovers in an airtight container in the fridge and serve warmed up the next day for a quick and easy breakfast.

• If you have a smaller crowd, feel free to cut the recipe in half. Use 2 small eggs and bake in a quarter sheet pan; alternatively, cook the batter on the stovetop in a buttered skillet as traditional pancakes (you'll get 12 to 15 pancakes).

• This recipe also makes the perfect muffin. My kids gobble them up! Simply mix the batter together, add any extras (chocolate chips, blueberries, shredded apple, etc.), and bake in muffin tins lined with cupcake liners, using the same directions as the original recipe. You'll get about 22 muffins with the full pancake batter recipe.

Have you ever met a kid who doesn't love pancakes? There's "cake" in the name, so I'm convinced the answer is a hard no! All three of my kids are pancake monsters. As you may know by now, I don't love baking and that's mainly because I don't like measuring ingredients. This is why we've been making surprise pancakes for years. Depending on which ingredients I have on hand, each day I concoct a new version of a pancake, using my general formula with slight variations. My Instagram followers are always asking for my pancake recipe, but I've never been able to share one because it changes daily. Well, this book was finally the push to perfect my pancake recipe and write it down at last. So, my friends . . . here you go. The best pancake in the world. It's healthy, it can be halved for a smaller batch, and it can be made the traditional method in a skillet or even be baked into the perfect healthy muffin. Top with fruit or chocolate chips or leave plain—no matter what, these pancakes are always perfection.

HOT TIPS (CONT'D)

- When we're shorter on time and need a quick pancake (and want to use up browning bananas), we opt for banana pancakes. I make these three times a week, and the kids love helping me make them (and beg for them), so the recipe needed to be quick. Mash together 4 bananas in a medium bowl. Whisk in 4 eggs, ½ cup whole-wheat flour, ½ teaspoon baking powder, a pinch of salt, and a drizzle of vanilla extract (optional). Fry in butter in a nonstick skillet with chocolate chips, then flip to cook the other side to make about 15 pancakes.

Fun fact: I've never made homemade pie dough, and I've made hundreds of pies over the years for my private chef clients! Let's just say I've always been a tad lazy, a bit savvy, and always creative in the kitchen. Why spend time making my own dough when I can buy it and make it look like my own? Keep this pie hack in your back pocket any time you want to make a sweet or savory galette, chicken potpie, or hand pies. I love making pie when I have fruit in the fridge that's starting to turn. I slice random combinations of fruit (using up whatever's in season) and bake it off, for a dessert that's easy to make and reduces food waste.

Fridge Cleanout Pie

MAKES 1 (9-INCH) PIE

1 Preheat the oven to 350°F.

2 Cut any larger fruit (plums, pear, apples, etc.) into thin slices and place into a medium bowl. Add the cornstarch, brown sugar, cinnamon, lemon zest, and salt. Mound the fruit mixture into one of the pie shells. Set aside.

3 Place a sheet of parchment paper (large enough to fit a standard baking sheet) on a work surface. Flip the dough from the second pie shell out of the tin (discard the tin) and spread it out on the parchment paper. Using a rolling pin (a can works well here too), roll the dough out a tad thinner, smoothing out the crinkled edges and making a thin, uniform round. Holding from under the parchment paper, lift up the dough and flip it onto the fruit-filled pie shell. Squeeze the edges of the top and bottom crusts together to seal and create a nice crimp around the edges. You can even use a fork to create a design once it's pinched and sealed.

4 Place the piece of parchment paper you used to roll out the dough on a standard baking sheet and place the pie on top. Brush the pie with the egg wash, getting it into all the grooves. Score an X with a knife in the center of the pie to create a vent for steam. Alternatively, you can punch out your favorite shape from the dough for the top crust before placing it on top of the fruit.

5 Bake on the middle rack for 55 to 60 minutes, until the crust is golden brown and the filling is bubbling. The more the filling oozes, the more rustic and beautiful this pie looks. Serve hot, with ice cream!

5 cups mixed fruit of choice such as plums, pears, apples, berries, pitted cherries, etc.

⅓ cup cornstarch

⅔ cup light brown sugar

½ teaspoon ground cinnamon

Zest of 1 lemon

Pinch of kosher salt

2 store-bought 9-inch pie shells in aluminum pans

1 large egg yolk, mixed with a splash of water, for egg wash

Ice cream, for serving

Switch It Up!

My number one goal is to show you how to be resourceful in the kitchen. Here you'll find inspiration for serving recipes from this book in completely new ways, which helps reduce food waste and keep you from eating boring leftovers. Mixing and matching staples is the Prep + Rally way! There are loads of ways to give recipes a new life with a little kitchen confidence and creativity. It's time to start switching things up and get more use out the recipes you already have. Below are some ideas to get you started.

- Asparagus (page 217) with 7-Minute Eggs (page 266) and Green Goddess Sauce (page 78)
- Sabich Bar (page 208) with Sunshine Kebabs (page 160) instead of eggs
- BBQ-Rubbed Chicken (page 32) with Salsa Verde (page 198) or Salsa Roja (page 177)
- Hawaij-Spiced Cauliflower (page 159) with Chimichurri Sauce (page 140) or Gremolata (page 176)
- Cabbage Wedges (page 175) with Ranch Dip (page 36)
- Kufte Smash Burgers (page 178) with Balsamic Jammy Onions (page 216) in buns
- Roasted Green Beans (page 114) served with Poke Marinade (page 98)
- Hawaij-Spiced Cauliflower tacos (page 159) with Salsa Roja (page 177)
- Cornbread muffins (page 74) with Chili (page 95)
- Hasselback Salmon (page 136) with Honey Mustard Sauce (page 220)

- Roasted Squash (page 135) served with Ponzu Sauce (page 98)
- Meatloaf (page 218) with Grown-Up Ketchup (page 178)
- Fried Rice Cakes (page 240) with Green Goddess Sauce (page 78)
- Green Enchiladas (page 200) using shredded chicken (see page 174), Rice (see page 197) and Salsa Verde (page 198) or Salsa Roja (page 177) as the filling
- Blend some jalapeño and an English cucumber into Hulk Soup (page 73) and serve chilled like a gazpacho
- Use Chimichurri (page 140) as a marinade for any steak or chicken and grill!
- Barbacoa Tacos (page 194) or Shawarma Chicken (page 55) with Salsa Roja (page 177) and Salsa Verde (page 198) for an extra fun taco night!
- Mushroom Cream Sauce (see page 158) as a pasta sauce with your favorite spaghetti or noodles
- Serve California Chicken Salad (page 256) as an appetizer topped with thinly sliced skirt steak (see page 194) instead of chicken
- Use Green Goddess Sauce (page 78) in a sandwich or to top grilled steak or grilled chicken
- Make egg rolls (page 43) with Barbacoa (page 194) instead of chicken
- Marinate thinly sliced chicken in Sesame-Lime Dressing (page 256) for an hour and grill! You can also make these into kebabs.

- Smashed Lemony Potatoes (page 59) dunked in Chipotle-Lime Crema (page 118)
- Pasta tossed in Citrus Butter (see page 220)
- Turn Cornbread into a fancier fruity dessert. See instructions on page 74.
- For a beautiful brunch spread, serve Roasted Squash (page 135) topped with labneh, Chimichurri (page 140), a fried egg, freshly squeezed lemon juice, and fresh pita for dunking
- Eggplant boats stuffed with Saucy Meat (page 138)
- Meatloaf (page 218) rolled into balls and baked
- Smashed Lemony Potatoes (page 59) with Gremolata (page 176)
- Smashed Tomato Sauce (page 118) simmered with fish or eggs like shakshuka

DIY Prep + Rally

I want to teach you the art of building your own Prep + Rally meal plan so you can keep going on your own. Making a menu for the week is one thing, but making a meal plan that can be smartly prepped in one day in minimal time with multiple serving options has a whole other set of rules.

Visit **prepandrally.com/diyprepandrally** for a free printable meal-prep template to use whenever you want to create your own customized menu. You can plug some of your favorite dog-eared recipes from this book and throw in some of your own personal family recipes. Hint: The Prep recipes from menus throughout

this book, and the Leftovers Remix (page 235) section will be very helpful here.

Of course, there is no one-size-fits-all meal plan, so feel free to get creative and make this your own. You can even prep a double-duty protein, one roasted vegetable, and one starch on Sunday, and that alone will give you some space to breathe throughout the week and fill in as needed! Build your meal plan based on your family's preferences, the season, what you're looking to use up in your fridge, and what you're physically able to tackle that day. Keep it simple and have fun with it.

Acknowledgments

Am I actually writing the acknowledgments for my cookbook? I truly never thought it would happen! This has been a total dream of mine since watching Giada De Laurentiis obsessively on the Food Network and deciding to give the food industry a wild shot. The path to get here hasn't been straight or simple and, gosh, have I hustled hard, but it's because of these stellar humans that you're actually holding this book in your hands:

To my editor, Sarah Pelz: It's been a wild ride but, boy, am I grateful for your guidance through to the finish line. I can't thank you enough for your kindness, patience, vision, and genuine enthusiasm for *Prep + Rally*.

To the talented team at Harvest Books and HarperCollins, including Melissa Lotfy, Marina Padakis Lowry, Emma Peters, Kimberly Kiefer, and Ivy McFadden. You took my manuscript and transformed it into the most gorgeous and easy-to-digest (pun intended) cookbook I thought only existed in my dreams. Thank you for your keen eye and for bringing this to life.

And to Mumtaz Mustafa: It's pretty wild how you designed my Dini Delivers logo five years ago and today, now working with Harvest Books, helped design this absolutely stunning cover. We've come full circle, and I'm beyond grateful you've been part of the journey from the very beginning.

Karen Murgolo: You are one of my OG supporters, and I can't thank you enough for all you've done. I'm eternally grateful.

To my agent, Alison Fargis: I could cry just thinking about this opportunity you've given me. From our first call, you've held my hand and shown such warmth and encouragement along the way. Thank you for believing in me and delivering far more than I could have ever dreamed.

Adeena Sussman: I've never met a more loyal, kind, and humble human. You've been my mentor through this cookbook world and always pushed me to reach higher. Your honesty and wisdom have hands down gotten me here today, and I will forever have you to thank.

To my incredible photography team: Everyone urged me to find a dream team. That is exactly what I found!

Ren Fuller: You are so incredibly talented, and I have you (and your dapple leaf) to thank for making this book so freaking gorgeous. Thank you for taking my vision and making it ten times better.

David Koung: Thank you for being so pleasant to have on set and for acting as our in-house label maker. I'll be selling them on eBay!

Marian Cooper Cairns: We scheduled our shoot around your schedule because I just knew I needed you to style these recipes. You are a wizard with food and make the best darn pimiento cheese out there!

Natalie Drobny: You're a boss in the kitchen and can Prep + Rally faster than anyone I've ever met, including myself.

Alicia Buszczak and everyone at The Surface Library: Thank you for taking me to prop heaven and for just getting me! Your hilarious stories kept my tummy hurting from laughter and kept the mood on set pure fun. You were such a joy to work with.

Aubrey Devin, Jaclyn Kershek, and Hannah Scheerer: Thanks for all your help during our shoot days! We couldn't have gotten through it all as fast without you.

Adena Frankel: You saved the day with wardrobe styling during some pretty strange times—I could have never gotten through this shoot without you! Thank you for your hustle, honesty, and for always being such a great friend!

Rivka Kantor: What started as a summer internship has grown into so much more. Your creativity, feedback, edits, positive can-do attitude, and smiley personality make the hectic workday enjoyable. I am so thankful for all that you do for Prep + Rally and my own personal sanity!

To all my recipe testers, including Sylvia, Sandy, Penina, Mariya, Ariella, Tunie, Allison, Simi, Aleeza, Tali, Itiya, Rebecca, Jennifer, Alison, Selina, Fay, Kailee, Shulamit, Chava, Liora, Seema, Liz, Laura, Elana, Julie, Rebecca, Sharona, Ilana, and Bassie: Thank you for your patience and honesty working through the recipes! Your voices were incredibly helpful, and I can't thank you enough for taking the time to help out.

To my foodie friends and friends in my personal life (or, in many cases, both): You know who you are, and I am so grateful to have you in my life. You lift me up, inspire me endlessly, and are always down for a phone call or glass of wine when I just need some grown-up time!

To my early Dini Delivers clients: You deserve a special shout-out because you've truly been there from the very start. Thank you for trusting me to cook for your twenty-five-person meals, for allowing me to make your special-occasion cakes, and for welcoming me into your home for all those years. You have helped me forge this path, and I will always remember those humble beginnings.

Deirdre and Tim Miller: My on-camera career began because of your belief in me. I am so grateful for our friendship through the years.

To my Prep + Rally tribe: I started sharing Prep + Rally meal plans on Instagram and cooking through them live together before gaining the confidence to design a website and make things official. I wouldn't be here right now had I not gotten the encouragement and support to just dive in and go for it! There aren't enough words on this planet to accurately describe how grateful I am for you and your support over the years. Without you, there is no Prep + Rally.

To my sisters: I feel so lucky to have you all in my life.

Aviva: Thanks for always cheering me on, making sure all your friends are following me, and for being the most honest and hilarious person to talk to.

Aliza: I've always wanted to be as good a cook as you. Thanks for letting me live with you while I was sorting out my life and for always sharing the best health/parenting advice. I learn so much from you.

Gila: thanks for doing my makeup for the shoot. You are such an insanely talented makeup artist and will always be my go-to for anything makeup- or fashion-related. I feel so grateful to live so close to you and be the beneficiary of your homemade chicken soup and juice tonics that you spoiled us with through all of our sicknesses this year.

Loni: I could have never survived those all-night, cooking-for-clients sessions without you. You filmed my first YouTube videos, taught me how to use Canva, stood in as a waitress and professional light hanger when I just didn't have anyone else, and always offered your time when work got super stressful. I laugh my hardest with you and feel so lucky to have such a special relationship.

To all my sisters-in-law and brothers-in-law: I feel so close to you all and love you like siblings. Special shout-out to my sisters-in-law, who are always encouraging and willing to drop anything for me at any time.

To my parents-in-law, Mishelle and David: Thank you for lending me your kitchen for my first sizzle reel (you were there from the very start!) and for genuinely loving me like a daughter even though I eat kale and can't re-create your potato kugel to save my life. Love you guys!

Dad: You've always pushed my creativity, given me a boost when I wanted to throw in the towel, and encouraged me to take the wild path that somehow got me here. We've always had such similar personalities and enjoyed doing all creative things together like designing the Prep + Rally cutting board! You truly make me feel like anything in life is possible. I am endlessly inspired by your abilities and can't thank you enough for giving me such a unique upbringing that ultimately landed me here. I love you so much!

Mom: You are the most energetic, fun-loving, and easy-going person I've ever met. You've always welcomed me into the kitchen to make messes, experiment, and play with food— I wish I could be that cool and relaxed with my own kids! Thank you for giving me the freedom to explore and find my way while showing so much love and encouragement. You are a supermom and I will forever try to be like you when I grow up.

Andi, Jolie, and Solomon: I feel like the luckiest mama in the world. Thanks for putting up with me and giving me the space to dream big while still being your mama—the juggle is real! You guys taste-tested every single recipe in this book, and your itty-bitty stamps of approval kept me pushing along. This book is truly our collective work, and I couldn't have asked for better partners in crime.

Mike: You vouched for me way back in Aaron's office, well before I knew what I was even capable of, and you haven't stopped believing in my vision since. You give me confidence, always know how to put my nerves at bay, and encourage me to push forward though the many highs and lows. Thank you for your honesty, your ~~unsolicited~~ business consulting, for encouraging me to "keep doing what you're doing," and for being the support system that got me through the final pages of this book. I become a better person daily because of you, and feel so lucky we get to do life together. I love you, Piggy!

Index

Note: Page references in *italics* indicate photographs.

About the Author

Dini Klein is a food host, recipe developer, former private chef, and founder of the Prep + Rally family meal-prep service.

Prep + Rally was Dini's solution to getting a wholesome dinner on the table on those busy weeknights when juggling mommying and work life felt almost impossible. Her system and uniquely designed meal plan structure now help thousands of busy families all over the world get through the week stress-free.

Dini has created food content for brands such as Walmart, Starbucks, WW International, PopSugar, Barilla, Campbell's, and more. Her work with Tastemade airs on Roku, Amazon, and Apple TV, and she's appeared live on KTLA, the Hallmark Channel, KSDK, and the CW sharing the Prep + Rally method. Her recipes have been published in cookbooks such as *Coffee, Dawn to Dusk* for Starbucks and Tastemade, and *The Pediatrician's Guide to Feeding Babies and Toddlers*. Dini has been featured in the *Wall Street Journal* and on Goop, and she's on a mission to help every busy family enjoy more and stress less with the Prep + Rally system.

Dini and her husband, Mike, live in Los Angeles with their three kids, Andi, Jolie, and Solomon.

Be sure to follow @prepandrally on all social media platforms and visit prepandrally.com for lots more meal prep inspo, cooking tips, and oodles of unfiltered family fun!